ROGUES . . .

. . . AND RUNNING DOGS

ROGUES . . .
. . . AND RUNNING DOGS

D. Brian Plummer

TIDELINE

British Library Cataloguing-in-Publication Data
A catalogue record for this book is available from
the British Library

ISBN   978-1-906486-34-1

First Published 1981
Second Impression 2009

©Kelvin S McCulloch 2008

Tideline Publications Promotions

49 Kinmel Street
Rhyl
Denbighshire
LL18 1AG

Digitally printed in the UK by Fineline Printing & Stationery Ltd.

CONTENTS

BY THE SAME AUTHOR

The Jack Russell Terrier, Its Training and
Entering

Modern Ferreting

Tales of a Rat Hunting Man

Illustrations and
Photographs
of the Dogs
written and described
in this Book

A FINE COLLECTION OF TYPICAL MIDLAND LAMPING LURCHERS

BEAR—THE AUTHOR'S NOTED FOX HUNTING LURCHER
A SALUKIE/COLLIE/DEERHOUND HYBRID

KEITH QUIMBY'S BEAUTY
A DEERHOUND X GREYHOUND X GREYHOUND HYBRID—A NOTED HARE KILLER

THE AUTHOR'S NORFOLK LURCHER
A GREYHOUND X COLLIE X GREYHOUND HYBRID

THE ENGLISH BULL TERRIER

A Whippet/collie hybrid
An excellent 'lamping' dog

A Bull Terrier/greyhound lurcher

A FINE COLLECTION OF TYPICAL MIDLAND LAMPING LURCHERS

BEAR—THE AUTHOR'S NOTED FOX HUNTING LURCHER
A SALUKIE/COLLIE/DEERHOUND HYBRID

BORDER COLLIE

BEDLINGTON TERRIER

BARNEY ENCOURAGED THE FERRETS AND PUPPIES TO DRINK
FROM THE SAME DISH

HE WOULD POINT TO A HOLE AND THE DOG WOULD MARK ONLY THAT HOLE

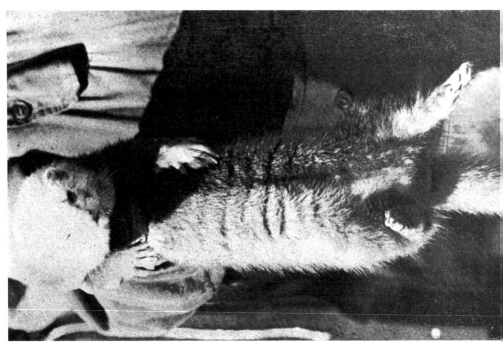

BILLY USED A HUGE ONE-EYED POLECAT HOB

WE SET TOO AND NETTED EVERY HOLE ERNIES DOG HAD MARKED

SALUKI

THE WORKING BEARDED COLLIE
—AN IDEAL STARTING POINT FOR THE ALL-ROUND POACHING LURCHER

THE SCOTTISH DEERHOUND

Foreword

A criticism of my book would be that it lacks a central theme, for there is a hiatus between the two parts. It is deliberately disjointed, for though I find lurchers little short of fascinating, I find their owners even more interesting. This is not meant to be a book on legitimate coursing—for I know of very few lurcher men who do not poach. My book is therefore about the more "seedy" aspects of lurcher owning. Poachers are fascinating people—the risks involved in the game are great and the profits small. True we have progressed from the time when the poaching of seven rabbits brought a sentence of ten years deportation to Australia. True magistrates rarely pay much attention to the grim game laws of the 1830's which were passed to ensure that the exploited poor stayed in the "dark satanic mills and left the game of the industrial tycoon masters strictly alone. Poaching is still a risky business however, for many of the magistrates are the descendants of those 19th century land owners, and have an inborn dislike of the poacher who wanders across forbidden fields raping the land of its game. Thus under our present chaotic legal system, housebreakers receive probation, muggers receive treatment but the convicted poacher receives a stinging fine.

I, therefore, dedicate this book to the poaching running dogs —and the rogues who own them.

ROGUES . . .

CHAPTER 1

An Interest Begins

Bear was not the first lurcher I owned. I once owned, no owned is the wrong word, a honey coloured, rough coated bitch called Claire. How I came by her was strange, and though I cursed her lack of loyalty often enough, when she died it nearly broke me in two, though strangely she had little affection for me, and basically I felt nothing for her.

Unlike all the fantasy type lurchers one reads about, who were born on gypsy camps from dubious ancestors, Claire's origin was well known. She was born in the kitchen of a council house in Dawley, and her dam was a mean, vicious collie cross greyhound bitch who had been a meat provider for the family for years. She had been a model hare dog in her youth, and would still take the unwary hare by an almost fox-like stalking. As her speed began to wane she was used to hunt rabbits at night. She was a useful lamp dog: quiet, obedient with a distinct distrust of strangers. Belle (the lurcher bitch) would kill fox as eagerly as she caught rabbits, and when her owner was prosecuted and convicted of poaching on the land belonging to the secretary of the local fox hunt, he took Belle and killed or ran off every fox just before the hunt was due to hunt the country. Sid Conners, Belle's owner, was a peculiar man. He thought nothing of poaching every form of game, and little of robbing factories or shops, but when I first started teaching in that area, and earned enough to keep a respectable rat just about alive, I left my monthly £44 (seems pitiful now and was pitiful then) on my sideboard and I think Sid would have starved rather than look at it.

Sid was a jobbing labourer, working when and where he pleased. He made most of his money by lamping and ferretting rabbits. When myxamatosis came to our area Sid's orders fell off rapidly, for someone had put the story about that some woman had contracted myxamatosis, and the meat eating world became decidedly anti-rabbit. Belle still hunted them but orders and rabbits became steadily less. Myxied rabbits are easy to catch and just sit out waiting to be killed. Sid dropped me the myxied carcasses for my dogs and ferrets and I confess I was so pushed for money that I ate many myself. Although Sid's orders for rabbits became less, there was other very saleable game not too far away. Belle was nearly twenty-six inches tall and had begun to thicken as she slowed up, but she would fight the devil himself, and fearned nothing. Her courage was to be her undoing in the end.

One day Sid brought me some liver—a whole liver in fact. At first I thought he had killed a sheep but on examining the liver my training as a biologist came up with the correct label—roe deer. Sid had found a herd that he had decided needed culling. In fact, Sid Conners hunted them nearly to extinction. He ran them nightly with Belle who, old as she was, entered into the hunt with great enthusiasm. If Sid had lived two hundred years ago he'd have been a candidate for hanging or maybe deporting. I looked at his huge catholic family and smiled. Everyone in Botany Bay would have probably had the same surname—Conners.

Deer don't give up without a fight, and when down not only do they scream fit to wake the dead, or the nearest game warden, but they kick like hell. Belle caught one of these hefty kicks and the tiny hooves broke her shoulder and front leg. Sid brought her to me and although I patched her up and put her leg in a splint, I am no vet and I knew she would never run again.

She never 'got right'. Her speed had gone, and after a hard run her front leg seized up. Many lurcher men would have put the cripple down, but, as Sid said, the breeding was there. She came near season and Sid began looking for a mate. There is a saying among lurcher men that one should not mate two lurchers together, and I suppose there is more than a grain of truth in the statement. I have seen many ugly lurchers that looked like scrawny collies and even lightly built mastiffs. When in doubt mate to a greyhound is an old and useful adage. A greyhound had to be the mate for Belle, and God knows there were enough about. One huge, black pied male greyhound lived just four doors away from Sid but Sid didn't reckon it good enough for Belle. He made a deal with a shifty character who 'walked' greyhounds from a local licensed track. One day a magnificent fawn dog arrived at Sid's house—'borrowed' for a night. After much fuss and bother the dog mated Belle. Nine weeks later Belle produced a litter, a smooth brindle dog and two honey-fawn, rough coated bitches. My story now takes up with one of these bitches.

Sid sold Claire to his brother Dan, big as a house, strong as a bull and gentle as a lamb. That is, when he was sober. When he had even a tiny amount of drink, a violent Mr. Hyde came roaring out of this man. I've heard construction workers say that they'd seen Dan take a pub apart, and his wife complained bitterly about the smashed furniture that littered the floor after Dan had a good night " on the beer ".

One day a very bruised and battered Dan appeared on my doorstep with Claire on the lead. " Would you like to borrow Claire on an indefinite loan?" I explained that I was strictly a terrier man, and had no use for lurchers. Dan damned nigh burst into tears. " Can't you see, you bastard, I'm giving her to you. I'm going away ". Dan had had a particularly good week on the town site they now call Telford and he had nearly a hundred pounds in his pocket; he had left his giant excavator, whistled up Claire and headed for the nearest pub. People still talk of the damage he did, and when the police arrived he went beserk. Screaming, cursing and kicking, he'd been taken into custody some eight miles away. He had returned home to find wife and children gone for good, but Claire, very wet and bedraggled, at the gate. Dan had wrecked pubs before and he knew he was " going down " for a very long time, particularly as he had done an arresting police officer considerable damage. Dan was in tears as he handed me Claire and her lead and walked down the lane away from my cottage. Looking down at the whining dog I knew she felt the same way as Dan. Few people loved this schizophrenic giant. Claire did.

Lurchers change hands fairly readily. The greyhound blood in their make-up makes them readily accept new owners and most settle down in new homes within a matter of hours. Claire was different. At first she refused to eat, and her hip bones showed through before she condescended to take food from me. When I let her run free, she headed for home. I think I fetched her back from that empty house in Dawley times without number, and when she was forced to settle she did so with a heavy heart.

I think I must have had Claire for about eight months. When
we hunted she was superb. No hedge was too high for her to
jump. No cover too thick for her to penetrate. She had a peculiar
gift when her keen eyes spotted an out of range hare. She would
" walk up " the feeding hare with the stealth of a cat. When the
hare began to notice the movement she froze. When she came
into range she took him with a lightning rush. Time dims memory
and bad dogs look a little better after a few years, but I think Claire
was the fastest lurcher I have ever seen. She was a gentle bitch
who was afraid of the local farm cat which ruled the woods around
my cottage. One day she surprised a fox that stood facing her
hissing and threatening, more feline than canine. I encouraged
her at it, but she merely wagged her tail and trotted back to me.
Claire just didn't like trouble. Rabbit and hare were different.
They offered no opposition and she regarded them as fair game.
To the reader she must have seemed the perfect lurcher. She
wasn't. When I took her hunting near my smallholding she was
well behaved. When we came near to places she had hunted with
Conners she remembers and headed for her old home. No amount
of shouting would stop her. I would find her crouched by the
gate of Conners old home. I confess I sometimes thrashed her
as I was driven mad by her ill-placed loyalty to her former master.

The 1962-63 winter was already looming on the horizon and
the weather changed suddenly. The unfallen leaves froze and
crumbled to dust when touched. Things were desperate as I still
earned my pathetic £44 per month. My salary was gobbled up by
my livestock, and I was now hunting in earnest to stay alive. By
mid-winter the snow had frozen like rock and Claire coursed rabbits
and hares across the unyielding crust of the frozen snow. They
were half-starved, wretched creatures, barely a third of their normal
weight. Woodpigeons staggered across the fields too weak to fly.
the ground became so hard that it was impossible to ferret as I
could not peg a net. When I tried to use my old polecat hob the
rabbits were too weak to bolt. The sixteen acres of rock and
scrub my estate agent had euphemistically described as a smallholding teetered on the edge of bankruptcy One day a roe buck
tangled in my barbed wire and my terriers pulled it down and
killed it, watched all the time by my puzzled Claire. I gralloched
him. No, gralloched implies wastage and we wasted nothing for
my dogs were desperate for flesh.

I had visions of it being the dreadful Viking Fimbul winter,
the winter to prelude the end of the earth, for March came and
the winter tightened its icy grip still further. When the last scraps

of deer had gone life hit a very low ebb for me. I had caught all
the game for miles around and I had to poach farther afield. I
began moonlight walks around Dawley hunting the rabbits and
hares that had survived the winter cold but still too weak to out-
pace even a terrier. One night I made a fatal error and hunted
Claire within a mile of her own home. She ran a hare, leaped a
hedge and chased it into the road. Then, in the still of that icy
moonlight night, I heard the squeal of brakes and the sound of a
body hitting a vehicle. I ran to the hedge and found a puzzled
articulated vehicle driver examining all that had been left of Claire,
for she was nearly sheared in two. Curiously the hare was also
dead as Claire was close on it when the collision occurred.

She had carried me through that dreadful winter supporting
me and my livestock. She had, in fact, given me all she could
except her affection, for I believe she lived only for the return of
her giant.

How to tell Conners was hard. Every letter allowed out of
prison was sent to me—always with questions of Claire. He never
even asked about his wife and children. I sent him a simple note,
telling him death was instantaneous and Claire had felt no pain,
but I had visions of a huge man tearing out the bars of his cell,
fortifying himself with a bottle of whisky and dismembering me.
Strangely it never happened. I never heard from him again. I
returned to his brother's home a few months ago and found out
why. Dan had died in prison and the coroner's verdict had been
cirrhosis of the liver, probably brought about by heavy drinking.
Maybe doctors can be correct about the cause of death, but I have
a nagging doubt that the loss of Claire contributed to his passing.
Such events wound the soul and are not revealed by autopsy.

My Fimbul winter ended. My holding went bankrupt and
had to be sold. I watched with a sad heart as the " For Sale "
notice was nailed up at the gate. It was the saddest time of my
life. I said Goodbye to England, and for a number of years
forgot about lurchers.

CHAPTER 2

Barney Lewis

I have always been a solitary person, and I feel decidedly unhappy and cramped when I go into a city. The army, and thirty-
two men to a billet, nearly suffocated me and my two years of
National Service crawled by at a snail's pace. My college days
were equally claustrophobic and unpleasant. The vast crowds of
students, the droves of rugby players who regarded me as some
sort of odd ball straight out of the gloom of Thomas Hardy
sickened me. Within a month of going to college I realised I
would be as much at home in the teaching profession as I would
be in the front row of the chorus of the Ziegfield Follies. Life to
my simian classmates meant rugby, rugby, rugby and as I have
always detested any form of team game I felt decidedly out of
things. I was labelled an anachronism by both students and
lecturers and left to my own devices. I came very near to leaving
college at the end of the Christmas holidays and then fortune
smiled on me and I met Barney Lewis.

At the end of my first term I was becoming very pessimistic
about my future. Through my own solitary disposition I was not
getting on with my college associates, and as I wanted to get out of
all scholastic commitments, I obtained a holiday job on a farm
near Newport. The farm was largely arable and I spent my time
hacking cabbage and kale which was very therapeutic for my mental
condition. All the crops were taking a bit of a beating from the
rabbit population, for these were the days before myxamatosis
had reduced the rabbit population to practically zero. In order to
curb the ravages of the rabbits the owner had given the shooting
rights to a bunch of local boys who had bought a few shotguns
and a springer spaniel. They had made little impact on the rabbit
population but had broken fences, left gates open, and had run
the kale so flat that it looked like the practice grounds of J. C.
Bamfords. Eventually he had to give in and employ a professional
rabbit catcher. I had heard much of Barney before he came, about
his wonderful gift of setting snares and his use of illegal gins, about
the prowess of his ferret and the running ability of his dogs. I
expected a hybrid between a James Fennimore Cooper hero and

Joe Louis. When he did turn up he was a bit of a disappointment. He was an insignificant, gingerhaired man with a straight out of the crypt pallor of a man who was a fugitive from a blood transfusion. Looks often belie ability. Barney was the best rabbit catcher I have ever met, and his teaching stood me in good stead when I finally rebelled against society, quit teaching and lived off the country.

Barney was from tinker stock. His father had come to this part of the country some fifty years before in horse drawn caravans. It took a long time for the Lewis family to settle and ameliorate their thieving ways, and an even longer time for the locals to accept the family. His father had been a bit of a character, and had fought as a useful flyweight at the booths under the name of Gypsy Lewis. He had been an artful, aggressive little man, ever eager to pit his wits against all comers. Once he had stolen some horses from the miners in the nearby valleys and sold them at the Gloucester fair. The miners had waited for him to come home, his pockets full of money and drunk as a lord. Two had fitted a noose of barbed wire around his neck and towed him round a field. The wire had cut into his vocal chords and for ever after he whistled when he spoke. Tinkers expected savage punishments if they were caught and never considered legal action. Barney, whose real name was Bernard Elisha Saul Lewis, grew up in a caravan and states that as a child he frequently suckled their nursing lurcher bitch! He could read and write after a fashion for he had seen the last years of the first world war and most of the second and had been involved on a compulsory education programme. Some of this education, but not much, had stuck, and though I had to write his letters for him he frequently browsed through his one and only book " Autobiography of A Super Tramp " by W. H. Davies— (The hobo poet who often met and talked with his father).

I taught him to read properly and he taught me—well just about everything I know. More important still he convinced me that I should stay on in college and take my finals.

The college sports afternoons were sheer hell for me. I have never been sports orientated and I dislike watching rugby and football. The chance of going on a poaching expedition with Barney was well worth the possible chance of suspension. Furthermore when I returned to college that January, I was determined to supplement my grant with a spot of rabbit-catching and I learned incredible poaching dodges from Barney. I learned to set a long net properly and to expect an amazing variety of game enmeshed in its net at the end of the drive. I learned how to skin rabbits so that the skins, as well as the flesh, were saleable. At that time the wild rabbit skins fetched a fair price at felt making factories, better than tame rabbit skins, for the earth and urine of the warren make minute chemical changes in the skin, so that the pelt is more suitable for felt making. One of the college cleaning ladies once reported me to the college principal, as I had a two foot pile of dry pelts in my locker and they stank. He gave me a quaint old fashioned look and then retreated into his Roman history book— different people different ways.

After a while I became very efficient at "placing" a term that I've only ever heard from Barney. This involves coming up quietly between the feeding-out rabbits and their warrens. A heavy ball, rolled up newspaper, is pushed about a foot into the holes and jammed with wood. Every hole is treated that way. When the hunter is 'good and ready' he goes in front of the rabbits and claps his hands, or merely shows himself. The effect is electrifying. The rabbits race back to the warrens. When they dive down to the apparent safety of their holes however, the rolled up paper stops them getting too far down and they merely wait, crouched against the paper, for the hunter to reach them out of the holes. If one is a silent sort of person who has a well trained dog who will not take off after the feeding bunnies, or worse still "give tongue" then this method can produce some useful hauls. Unfortunately the survivors "educate" to this method and take to feeding near the warrens during daylight hours only venturing far out during dusk. Psychologists tell you rabbits are among the lowest intelligence in the mammal world. Hunters will tell you otherwise.

This method is not, however without its dangers. Once we were "placing" on a warren which lay near a river bank in Caerwent. We placed our brown paper parcels on the holes and crept back. Barney's whippet bitch began to edge in on the feeding rabbits, who, not being particularly frightened, merely loped back to their holes. We walked towards the bank and drew out a rabbit or so killing them quickly with a rabbit punch on the back of their necks. Nell, Barney's whippet, marked one hole with an air of apprehensive anticipation. I immediately thought that a whole crop of rabbits were lying just out of reach of the whippets long muzzle. I flashed my hand into the hole and experienced the most exquisite agony I have ever known. I withdrew my hand from the hole with some difficulty. On one of my fingers was a huge doe rat swollen with young. She had scampered back to the warren with the feeding rabbits. The "bite" was agonising and made all the more horrendous by the fact that the rat watched me, its black beady eyes sparkling with terror. Everytime I moved, the terrified beast tightened its grip. For the first time since I had know him I realised I was not going to get any help from Barney, for I glanced up and his pasty face had gone a whiter shade of pale. Both Barney and the whippet had one thing in common, both were terrified of rats. It gave me a horrid feeling that John Donne's quote: " No man is an island " was untrue. I was; I'd get no help from Barney or the dog. Excruciating as the pain was I think I felt more hurt because I realised my hero had a tragic flaw in his personality. " Throw your mattock across ", I whispered. The terrified Barney slowly came to life and slid the razor sharp mattock across towards me. I moved slowly, trying not to frighten the rat into gripping even more tightly. I raised the mattock and dealt the beast a sharp blow and nearly severed the head from the body. It gave one ghastly convulsive tightening of its jaws that sent its teeth grinding against the bones of my finger, and then released hold and expired. Blood oozed from the chisel bite and my bruised finger began to swell visibly. When we arrived at Barney's house he slapped on a nasty green mess—a " simple " to prevent the wound from going bad. It didn't work. My thumb swelled like a balloon. I'd have to see the college doctor, but how does one explain a rat bite on his hand, when one has booked out from college to go to a local library for some books on Froebel!

Barney rarely talked about his past and I knew very little about him, until one day I helped him fill in some forms for a gamekeeper's job in the Grampians. As I filled in the form I was aware that I had missed out four years from Barney's life. " What were you doing during those four years Barney?" I asked. " Four years " came the laconic and sheepish reply. Barney began to explain. He had once been a Peter Man—criminal slang for a man who " blew " safes. Barney had become an expert with the highly unstable, explosive nitroglycerine. He had palled up with a nervous, young thief who was just about as unstable as the explosive, and blown a safe in a nearby town. Later the two of them had been picked up stealing eggs from a local poultry farm, and in his panic, Barney's tense young associate had " coughed " for the safe job as well. Barney went away for the next four years. Several people who have " done time " state that the long term offender develops a pallor that never leaves them. Suddenly I understood Barney's complexion. In the four year gap, I wrote " government service " and passed the application form back to him.

Barney was an expert ferreter. In spite of his mortal fear of rats, he had no qualms about ferrets. His were the tamest hobs and jills I have ever seen. He would even put a finger in their mouths to pull out a piece of putrid meat they had picked up. He always encouraged his ferrets and puppies to drink from the same dish and never stopped a ferret punishing a boisterous puppy. In spite of the local belief that if a ferret was fed blood it would kill and lie up, Barney fed his only on rabbit offal and heads. Most of the locals fed bread and milk slop and found Barney's feeding methods bewildering. He laughed at these ideas and said " When God " gid " them these wicked eye teeth it weren't to mouth bread and milk ". If they are fed bread slop they tend to crave for the vitamins that are found in meat and when they get on a rabbit they go absolutely barmy for the vitamins that are found in meat. Of course they kill and gorge themselves. They then lie up and people call them useless. " People who feed bread and milk to ferrets are always strong ". They've got to be as they are always digging to get them out. Barney had his own ideas on getting a ferret to release a grip on a human finger. " They know they've made a mistake as soon as they bite " said Barney, " they hang on to prevent falling. Put your hand on the ground and they'll release after they're certain they won't fall ". We once watched a young blood in shooting costume and festooned with cartridge belts performing all sorts of barbaric practices to get a ferret off. Barney took hold of the young man's hand and placed it on the ground. The ferret released his hold quite quickly and sniffed the bitten hand. The young fellow was so pleased that he didn't ask what we were doing poaching his shoot.

Barney's ferrets were bred in rather tatty cages but as soon as they were weaned they were turned loose in a heavily boarded yard. It was nearly impossible for a ferret to escape, but some did. I learned the simple homely wisdom of denying that a ferret had escaped if someone accosted me. Usually people would come up to Barney and politely ask " Have you lost a ferret?" Barney would look blank, pretend to check his ferrets and always answer: " No ". " It's dollars to doughnuts that if a man brings back a ferret, it has killed his chickens or ducks ", said Barney. You may loose a £1 worth of ferret, but if you claim it back you'll pay a lot more in damages. I was to discover the truth of this some years later. If a ferret gets out, and you own up, as I did, then even the mangy fleabitten fowl it has killed will suddenly blossom into champion birds worth breath-taking prices. Furthermore it is easy to break dogs to fowl, but impossible to break a ferret. The ferret is a tamed polecat and the word polecat comes from the French la poule—a hen, for polecats are habitual hen killers. Forgetting

Barney's advice and owning up to the loss of a ferret cost me £62 some twelve years later. Once when asked if he had lost a ferret Barney had replied: " No, but if you come across an eleven foot alligator that's mine ". The looks on people's faces when he said strange things like that had to be seen to be believed.

Barney bred a tiny, frail strain of what can only loosely be classed as whippets. On reflection I think someone must have found an Italian greyhound some years back and crossed the animal with a small whippet. He had bred so many that he knew exactly where to find a dog to mate to any bitch brought to him. They were some of the most fragile little dogs I have ever seen. Most were small enough to get to ground and I have seen several bolt foxes though they would have been reluctant to course one. They were not as nesh as they appeared however and would crash through the thickest bramble cover after a rabbit. Very few would even look at a rat. A sure sign that there was a rat in the hole is the dog would refuse to enter. I wish I had know this fact before I received that hellish bite.

Like all real McCoy hunters, rabbit exterminators and poachers, Barney's dogs were all superbly trained. He would point to a dog to stay by the nets while ferreting and the dog stayed and watched only that hole. If a rabbit bolted, hit the nets and tangled, the dog wouldn't look at it. If it slipped the nets and bolted the dog had it in a flash. His dogs never killed but merely held the rabbit, retrieving it alive and unharmed. Once a hare got up and one of his smaller dogs grabbed it. The hare towed the dog across the field. Some wit said " Stop it, Barney, the hare's running off with your dog ". It failed to hold the hare and the beast ran away screaming. Barney only sold rabbits and his dogs were part of the trade and they were only required to catch rabbits. No one could have said they were general purpose lurchers.

My time at college came to an end and I passed my finals which would not have strained the mind of an orang utang and left the district. Barney did not get his gamekeeper's job and remained in Gwent. I never saw him again. Once when my holding had gone bankrupt and I was experiencing the depths of despair I returned to look up Barney. My despair was increased not dispelled. Barney had had a heart attack and lost the use of his neck muscles and one side. He was virtually a cripple and took a lethal overdose rather than live a half-life. A man called Homer once said, " A year in the lifetime of a sheep is only equal to a moment in the life of a tiger ", and Barney was a pathetically thin, anaemic, but never shabby tiger.

CHAPTER 3

Hardy

"The main reasons for the breakdown of my marriages are bred down grews, black reds and women—in that order". This was the way one of my favourite characters began the story of how his three marriages had broken down and why each and every wife had described him as " lunatic " and taken to the hills. Hardy —what an incredible character, met his death in a Yorkshire coal face.

I first came to know Hardy—a nickname not a surname or Christian name—when I started to develop an interest in Medieval bloodsports for a teaching project in which I was engaged. I was at that time employed at a school that was run by a Dickensian headmaster who, bristling with dignity and religion, had set about to " clean up " the timetable which meant that any topic which could have been interesting was immediately pruned until it became deadly boring. He would brook no lesson that even lightly touched on the violent aspect of life. As a result the lessons became bland and boring for the pupils and massive truancy began. Who could blame them for our head made us teach in a style that made the conflict between Harold and William at the Battle of Hastings seem like a brotherly meeting between two long lost " chums ". I had gone to Hardy's home on the unpleasant business of telling him that his son was one of the worst truants. He was a bright, lively boy who, with better teaching might have been an academic, but with the slop we were forced to serve under the guise of education, he just refused to attend school. Hardy lived in one of those long winding rows of stone built terraced houses that had been flung up with indifference for the workers at the end of the last century. They were all without character (or damp courses) and without exception the backyards and tiny gardens boasted pigeon " cots " or pens of poultry. I felt as if I had stepped back into my own childhood as I walked along that street. I knocked at the door of number 59, and was aware of the fact that the front of the house needed pointing and painting. I smiled almost apologetically as Hardy opened the door and thrust his huge distended abdomen towards me as if in defiance. I gingerly accepted his invitation to enter his whippet-filled house and felt trapped as he closed the door. Hardy was a huge man who had a well deserved reputation for being violent.

Once indoors with the last vestige of my courage gone, I glanced around the room. The usual mining household of my own childhood was not like this. Hardy's walls were literally covered with sporting prints. Duck wing game cocks spurred and blood-stained stood on the bodies of the fallen adversaries and crowed defiance to the world. Bull terriers locked in combat, their faces contorted with anguish and hate, twisted their bodies to get in a crippling stifle bite, and there hanging along the wall like a giant, grisly charm bracelet was a leather belt from which protruded a variety of cocking spurs. My curiosity soon overcame my apprehension and I stepped forward to touch the needle ends of the spurs. All were genuine. All were antique, though most showed signs of recent work. I came to one exquisite piece of death-making I recognised. "A Ross", I cried excitedly, fingering the sharp point and flicking the spur till it sang. I turned and said, "These were deadly spurs". They were made in Bloxwich and the workmanship was so good that they fetch a fortune in the "States". I had seen them advertised in two horrific periodicals called euphemistically "Grit and Steel" and "The Feathered Warrior". Hardy's face broke into a grin as he witnessed my infantile excitement, and for the three years I stayed in the Barnsley district he became my greatest friend.

As soon as Hardy bcame aware that I was not a member of the R.S.P.C.A. out to prosecute him for his sundry brutalities, and that I was far too scruffy to be a plain clothes policeman out to send him to hell for his outrageous hobbies, Hardy's character unfolded like a flamboyant painted fan. He was the essential antidote to my religious cadaver-faced headmaster, and without him I would have gone insane. The school in which I worked would have won any prize in killing the interest in anyone, and kids and staff trudged unwillingly to school each day. As soon as the 4.0 p.m. bell rounded the end of the day's boredom I raced to Hardy's house to find relief from the depressions brought on by that dreadful school.

Hardy bred and fought black/reds, a formidable strain of game chicken, that had been used for cock fighting before the Phonecians landed on our shores (Birds so game that they would fight on and even win a battle long after essential parts of their viscera had been removed by the slashing of their antagonists spurs). The police must have known of Hardy's macabre and bloody interests yet they left him very much alone. If they could have caught him, they would have prosecuted him, but it is very difficult for the police or anti-blood sport fraternity to penetrate the shadowy and "will o' the wisp" world of the cock fighter.

Hardy worshipped his birds. He fed them on only the best of grain and supplemented their corn diet with a sickly cake that smelled strongly of cheap draught sherry and just a hint of corruption and decay. He claimed that this secret mixture gave the bird courage and stamina to go on after they were badly lacerated in a fight. The fact that the birds were game enough to wolf down the horrid mess was proof enough of their bravery as far as I was concerned. Hardy frequently offered me a spoonful of this vile concoction but after I had ascertained that the mixture was probably the cause of his rotund shape and rotten teeth I declined gracefully.

He had one of the most amazing general knowledges I have ever encountered, and his collection of facts about bloodsports in general and cock fighting in particular was nothing short of incredible. I once persuaded him to come to talk to my class on the subject of cock fighting and its long and unpleasant history. He would have fascinated my class who relished a feast of gore, but my headmaster vetoed the suggestion. To our Dickensian head, who sat white haired and awe inspiring in his study preaching "God is love" and practising savage flagellism, Hardy was an anathema. It turned out that during his student teaching days he had taught Hardy who had rejected the Bible thumping and ran away from school, after attacking our head.

To me, however, Hardy was far from anathema and his place became a regular Shangrila of interest. I sat listening to his tales of cock fighting, poaching and dog racing until the small hours of the morning. Our champion staff room bore, a title won amidst savage competition, and who could have made a ringside seat at the Battle of Waterloo seem a bit of a drag, warned me often of the dangers of frequenting Hardy's house, and would whisper confidentially "The head knows all about it you know", to put me off my fat and fascinating friend. Thank God he failed.

Hardy's premises stank of strange odours. The obscene smell of cocking cake fought a desperate battle to vie with and overcome the odour of sheep's paunch. His backyard (equally smelly) was a muddy morass of trampled earth and dog urine with just a hint of

slivers of sheeps' skulls, for Hardy bred a hybrid whippet greyhound which raced at the local track under the misnomer of pure
bred whippet.   During the years following the first world war
whippet racing was popular, and the right racing blood easy to
obtain, but the war years and the post war food rationing put an
end to the sport.   During the late 1950's however there was a
revival of interest in the sport, but there were just not enough of
the real McCoy racing whippets about.   The show bred whippets,
glamorous though they appeared, lacked the fire and guts of the
racing dogs and their times were poor.   On to the Northern scene
came Hardy, brainwave in head and tiny coursing greyhound in
hand.   Hardy mated this tiny aggressive greyhound bitch to the
best racing whippet dog available and bred a strain of dog that he
called ' 'bred down grews " that wiped the boards with show
whippets racing at the local tracks.   True some were obviously
greyhound bred, and went to coursing homes as they were too large
to race at the whippet tracks, but those who qualified for the title
" whippet " (under 30lbs.) took some beating.   Hardy had buyers
from as far afield as Kerry for his racing dogs and his bigger
dogs, which he sold as lurchers, were some of the best coursing
dogs around Barnsley.   He never had spare puppies and he had a
waiting list for both racing and coursing dogs.

The dreadful smell of the backgarden that housed both fighting cocks and whippets was a bone of contention between Hardy
and his immediate neighbours.   On hot days the stench resembled
a maggot factory in full production, and the neighbours had good
cause to complain.   One day Hardy had a visit from a public
health officer; a bright, smartly dressed young man who had " come
about the smell ".   Hardy immediately acted slightly insane and
began to speak in a dialect that even a died-in-the-wool Yorkshire
man would find hard to understand.   The public health man
listened with patience to Hardy's babblings nodding his well
groomed head as if he understood.   He took a pad from his pocket
wrote " Nutter " across one leaf and left.   Hardy had no more
visits.

On most days Hardy was reluctant to give away the secrets
of his success as a whippet racer.   One day he cleaned up sixty
pounds in bets at the track, and spent a wild and woolly night at
the local pub.   I returned to his place with a group of the locals
and the intoxicated and exhilerated Hardy spent four hours explaining his breeding programme to his group of spellbound eager
listeners.   " When war ended the real racing whippet blood had
gone for good and everyone sought ways of recreating the old fiery
whippet blood that would dash through hell for the wave of a

sock ", said Hardy. Many crossed whippets with very game
Staffordshire Bull Terriers and mated back to whippets until most
of the Staffordshire Bull blood had disappeared and all that
remained was the " sting ". Others used the more lightly built
Bedlington terrier on their whippets and you still see some whippets
with " slick " (Hardy's term for broken coats) running on tracks
today. " These breeders were daft. They were too stupid to see
that the show breeders had bred out the fire in the terriers, just as
they had bred out the " death or glory " in the whippet. I was just
as daft as they were once and I crossed " odds and sods " with
whippets to get the right stuff. They made good lurchers but they
were too slow for the track. " About this time ", he went on " there
was bad feeling about coursing so I was determined to see the
Waterloo Cup before the anti-blood sport people knocked it on
the head. When I was there I met a bloke who was keen to part
with a tiny coursing bitch. She'd been a real heller—killing sheep,
chickens, pigs, ducks and cats by the dozen. The bloke was at
his wits end what to do with her, so I took her off his hands. At
that time one of my mates owned a tiny rag dog (whippet) that won
most of his races because the other dogs were handicapped because
of their larger size. I mated this dog to my " grew " and kept back
the tiny ones. Since then I've been unbeatable on the rag dog
tracks. Furthermore ", he added, " if a show whippet gets too big
most breeders put them down. Most will just chase and refuse
to kill so they're damn all good for coursing. Mine will chase
and tackle out ". Most of Hardy's " whippets " were touchy to
break to sheep and poultry and were devils with cats inheriting
much of the killer instinct of their pathological matriarch. All of
Hardy's dogs would break their heart trying at hare and Fly, his
noted brood bitch, would bowl and probably kill a fox.

Hardy began training his puppies as soon as their eyes could
focus. He would toss in a piece of rag and tease the whippets with
it. They would squeal with excitement when they saw Hardy
approach with a rag. He would hang a piece of cloth in their
sheds just out of their reach. The young running dogs soon were
" rag " mad and would go berserk at a piece of cloth flapping in
the hedgerow. One day Hardy was excercising a team of young
hopefuls on the common, when a young woman from the local
training college passed by, her college scarf flapping in the breeze.
The three whippets snatched at the scarf and pulled the student
over. Hardy had great difficulty in explaining what had happened
to the screaming young woman.

In the district Hardy had the reputation of being " near
lunatic ". In his youth, his wild ways were the talk of the town,
and his mother went grey with his antics. He knocked round with

a group of lads who bred a type of Lakeland terrier and used them for fox and badger hunting and probably a bit of fighting on the side. One day Hardy had a live fox which he intended to sell to a man who bred Staffordshire Bull Terriers, and wanted to test his dogs' courage. He refused to pay Hardy, so Hardy found himself stuck with a live fox. He had been drinking heavily and went to the local greyhound flapping track, fox and sack on back. Here beer and boredom combined to give him inspiration. He tipped the fox out on the track just in front of the racing greyhounds. Pandemonium seems to be the word to describe what happened, and Hardy was barred from the track. Some time later he turned a live badger loose during the ladies night at the local working men's club and both women and men fainted as Brock turned over furniture and glasses. Even when middle-age had made him calm down, people still watched him to see what madness he had up his sleeve.

I came to know Hardy well, and I knew he was as sane as the next man, but one day I began to have doubts about his mental health and I had a sneaking feeling friend Hardy might have been a pervert. Hardy had a bitch that was a result of his first cross between a whippet and his coursing greyhound. She was a lean gaunt 40lb. dog, too big to race, so Hardy kept her as a poaching companion, brood bitch and competition dog with a difference. Fly and Hardy would go to Mexborough Public Lavatories, meet half a dozen other men and disappear inside. I had awful suspicions about Hardy but I needn't have worried. Fly was a wonderful jumper and for money bets, Hardy would take her inside the cubicles and jump her over the partition wall. He was most hurt and indignant when suspicious losers accused him of jumping her " off pan " and invited the doubting Thomas inside the cubicle to witness Fly's feats of athletic prowess. I often wonder how the occupants of the next cubicle must have felt when a forty pound whippet scaled the wall and came crashing down on them. Hardy would always take on bets on pay days and won as much as fifty pounds a time on Fly's lavatory cubicle feats. It was certainly an incredible performance for a bitch weighing only forty pounds to scale a high cubicle wall without a run.

Fly lived in with Hardy, slept in his bed, ate from his plate and went to the pub with him, drinking from the same glass. This last action was to be Hardy's undoing for Fly would become excited after two or three pints of shared beer and leap on the table excitedly, poking her nose into various beer and spirit glasses. All the miners knew her and tolerated Hardy's eccentric ways, but one day a student from Sheffield University collecting local colour or maybe just slumming it, came into the public bar. Fly, exhilarated by her beer, leaped on the table and nosed the student's drink. To be fair, the student was fairly patient and made a considerable effort to cover his beer, but Fly was persistent. Hardy laughed the incident off and said "She's just like one of the family ". " Oh yes ", said the student, " which one?" Hardy took a full minute for the insult to get through to him, but made up for lost time by nearly dismantling the poor young fellow. Hardy was charged with grevious bodily harm, and, as he was not a first offender by any means, he did " time ". While he was away the public health authorities swooped and made Hardy's brother Chris get rid of all the dogs and clear up the place. Hardy returned to a relatively clean and disease free house but within a month of his release, he had the back garden looking like a quagmire again and had retrieved the dogs Chris had given away. With regulations regarding dog breeding, sanitation and building, the Englishman's home can scarcely be regarded as his castle. Hardy's home was, and he was king in his own house when he was at home.

Hardy's pleasure was to go out on Sunday morning at first light and course hares. He never ate hares and always offered them to the farmers after he had poached them from their land. Few landowners objected to Hardy running hares on their land, he was such a likeable fellow. Fly, his dynamic jumping bitch, had an impressive haul of hares, by the time she retired, all taken on land Hardy regarded as his by right. One day an angry young man in shooting outfit and cheap double barrelled shot gun raced across to Hardy and challenged his " right " at gun point. With gun cocked and face red with anger the young man had stated that he was going to prosecute Hardy for poaching on a private shoot " Don't be daft, man ", said Hardy pushing the gun away. The gun went off and the young man seeing Hardy's anger rise dropped the gun and took off like a deer back to his parked M.G. Midget. With Hardy's huge bulk the young fellow was probably convinced that a charge of number six shot would have scarcely slowed him up.

Not only was Fly a noted jumper. In his cups Hardy was equally famous. Once in a village pub near Mexborough I found Hardy involved in a heated argument with some miners. I saw some money change hands and Hardy swayed his drunken way across to my table. " Come outside man and hold money ". Hardy, a huge hulk of a man, had been challenged to stand in an empty beer barrel and jump out keeping his feet together. It seemed an impossible task. I stood holding the money with my eyes closed and wondered as to whether Hardy would be able to make a living advertising hernia appliances. There was a grunt, a groan and a smack and Hardy leaped out of the barrel. I needn't have worried. Hardy had been a noted jumper in his youth and had been doing his barrel trick for a number of years.

Fly's jumping ability once nearly cost Hardy his life. Hardy had an allotment which had a garden shed. In the shed a pot bellied stove smouldered and Hardy would spend many hours crouched over the stove reading sporting periodicals and lurid paperbacks. Once a cousin of Hardy's from the same wild stock had lost a lot of money—his entire wage packet in fact—on Fly's jumping ability and to recoup his losses had backed "double or quits" against Hardy's barrel trick. Two weeks' wages down the drain and his wife had gone berserk. He found Hardy in the shed asleep. He locked the door and poured water down the stove pipe. The steam and carbon monoxide had damned nigh killed Hardy before he managed to kick the side out of the shed.

After three years I'd had enough of that dreadful school and I applied for a job in a country school further south. Just before I left Barnsley, Fly was put to sleep and the light went out of Hardy's life. I had found a maggot factory and obtained the ratting rights on the disgusting place. It was a haven for rats and I took several hundred a day with my team of terriers. Hardy listened to my tales of rat catching with interest "Like to try Fly at rats", he said almost to himself. That Saturday we went to the maggot factory with ferrets and spray guns that squirted petrol down the holes and when we exploded it, it made Fly jump out of her skin. She soon adapted and with a dainty and delicate flick of the head she killed several dozen rats. She was as agile as a ballet dancer and moved with incredible speed. Fly had enjoyed the day as much as Hardy and as dusk approached we packed up and went home after a highly successful day. A week later a worried Hardy appeared at the school gates "Come look at Fly, she's down". Fly had gone off her feet and her eyes and belly were a bright yellow. My own dogs were injected against the deadly Leptospiral jaundice which is carried by about half the rats of Britain but Hardy had never innoculated a dog. We called in a vet and he injected Fly with a massive dose of antibiotic, but Wiels disease is deadly. Fly died a few days later, a pitiful yellow wreck. It broke Hardy's heart.

It was the last day of term and I left that dreadful school. I never saw Hardy again. What a character passed away when he died. A genial eccentric giant who would eat hard boiled eggs, shells and all, like a giant Daniel Quilp just to make a child laugh and who was a genius at producing bred down grews. I missed Hardy when I came south.

CHAPTER 4

Billy Robbins Rogue Extraordinary

I know no man who deserved the title rogue more than Billy Robbins. He was utterly unscrupulous, totally amoral and completely fascinating. They just don't make rogues of Billy's sort anymore, and perhaps it is for the best.

When I left Barnsley I became interested in falconry, and as I disliked the pageantry and ostentation of the typical falconer I refrained from joining a falconry club and I learned my falconry from archaic and often inaccurate books. I obtained a home office licence for a buzzard, obtained a nestling from S. Wales and learned falconry through the mistakes I made in training him. He became so tame that he would come from half a mile when I shouted for him, but he was terrified of live rats and rabbits and utterly useless as a hunting bird. I was now eager to try the real McCoy (a bird that hunted, not a carrion eater like my buzzard) so I finally settled for the valiant and diminutive sparrow hawk. In those days a sparrow hawk was not easy to find. Dieldrin Aldrin and the other hellish chlorinatedhydrocarbons had thinned out the bird to near extinction. Furthermore, although they were protected birds, most gamekeepers regarded them as the scourge of game chicks, and shot them on sight. To obtain a licence for such a bird was out of the question, so I resorted to break or at least bend the law and get some gamekeeper to trap one for me. I then intended to train it out of the public eye and fly it, again illegally, at partridge, for a good sized female sparrow hawk could provide me with a considerable amount of sport. My first task was to find a gamekeeper and they were plentiful enough in the district.

Most keepers I met were quite open about the fact that they shot sparrow hawks on sight in spite of the fact they were protected by law, but not one of the gamekeepers had a clue how to trap a live sparrow hawk. Inspite of these setbacks I was still obsessed with the idea of getting my hawk and with memories of the bird trapper of my mining village, I set out to find a man who still trapped birds with illegal and grisly methods such as birdlime and padded gins. A keeper who lived near my cottage cleared his throat and spat in disgust, "You'll be wanting that sod Billy Robbins. Watch him, he's the worst rogue unhung. If you shake hands with him count your fingers when you get your hand back. He'll nick anything will Billie. Everything he touches is dishonest. Even his bloody budgie probably steals ".

On this note I set out to seek my legendary Robin Hood figure, who stole from rich and poor alike and kept it! I had only to mention Billy's name to one of my pupils to discover his address. " Cor, sir, he's fantastic. He's got birds, badgers, foxes, everything ". Clearly my class were impressed in fact they found this country vagabond a source of wonder. I was later to join Billy's band of admirers.

Billy lived in a scruffy cottage at the end of a long lane. Once the cottage had probably been pretty and picturesque. Billy had let it fall into a state of decay and disrepair. His garden was a mass of filthy packing-case sheds with urine scented earth between them, trampled to a malodourous mud. Foxes, badgers and even an otter cub peeked out from the gaps in the crates. The stench from the cages was almost unbelievable. Billy rarely cleaned out his livestock, and his interest in them seemed to stop as soon as he had trapped them. At the end of the garden was an aviary that housed almost every variety of British finch, which fluttered nervously above two feet of compacted bird muck. Not one was rung or aviary bred. Many were fresh caught, Billy was what was known as a dabhand at bird liming. He placed his multicoloured Judas call bird near a thistle patch and it lured in its unsuspecting brethren. Using a mixture of lime and linseed, and God knows what, he smeared the twigs around the thistle bed with his sticky mixture and waited. The finches flocked in to feed with their feathers clogged and sticky, they waited until Billy came along to claim them. Billy later sold his captures to finch breeders and even to an aviary in a big department store in a nearby town. Sadly many of Billy's captures died and it was not uncommon to to see Billy's huge hob ferret munching on the seven coloured carcass of a gold finch. Robbins wasted nothing.

As I gazed at the treasures Billy had filched from the country-side I was aware of a faint growling behind me. I turned quietly and found a lurcher with obvious collie blood snarling at my heels.

I had the feeling that if I had even dared to touch the aviary the
dog would have hamstrung me. As I stood petrified by the snarling dog, a soft spoken voice said " Do yer want something?" I
turned, a weedy, scruffily dressed little man with a ferretty face
had watched me come down the path. " Billy Robbins?" I asked
trying to force a smile. My questioner didn't even bother to
answer, and continued to stare at me. " I'd like to give you some
business " I went on. " I want a live, unhurt female sparrow
hawk ". I was about to explain that I wanted to train it for falconry
when Billy cut me short. " Don't catch birds—it's illegal ". The
aviary behind me proved that a lie, but I was out to do business
with Billy, not anger him. " Look ", I said quickly. " I teach
at the school by the " Big House ". If you do hear of a female
sparrow hawk in good feather, it's worth two quid to you ". I
watched Billy's twitchy, weasel face change slightly and was aware
that the offer of two quid had gone home. One week or so later
I was supervising the school dinner line when our buxom P.E.
mistress bounded up and said in mock rustic tones " Ee be thee
the tarrier master?" I knew immediately Billy had checked me
out, realised that I wouldn't shop him to the R.S.P.C.A. and had
trapped me my sparrow hawk. I raced out to the gate and found
Billy deep in conversation with two of our village hard cases that
had reduced my lessons to rubble week after week. They were
treating Billy with a respect that seemed totally foreign to them.

" Got what you want. Fetch it tonight " said Billy tersely
and left. I was about to thank him but he turned his back on me
and walked off. That night I went to Billy's cottage and was sold
a wild eyed, feather perfect sparrow hawk. " How did you catch
her?" I said, making no bones about my admiration for his
trapping prowess. " The two quid is for bird, not for trade
secrets " snapped Billy putting me in my place. He must have
had slight remorse about my obvious embarrassment and chipped
in " Hear you got a famous terrier ". At that time I owned a hard
bitten slashing fighting Russell Terrier as useful as he was ugly.
" How much yer charge to line my bitch?" I eyed his ugly cur
terrier that showed obvious collie influence. " Nothing " I replied
aware of the fact that if I had suggested a fee Billy would have
stolen the stud dog and returned it next day after it had served his
bitch. Thus began my somewhat fragile friendship with Billy
Robbins, the most extraordinary rogue I have ever encountered.

In Billy's world everything was for sale and if someone had
made him an offer for his consumptive haggard wife she would
have been wrapped up and sold. If a creature crawled, ran, swam
or flew, Billy could catch it. He made big profit using his large

one eyed hob ferret to catch live rabbits which he sold to the soulless undesirables that haunted the flapping tracks. These greyhound owners used these rabbits to " sharpen " a dog before a race, for the squeals of a dying rabbit are supposed to make a greyhound keener to run a clockwork hare. Billy's hob always drove rabbits into the nets. It never killed underground. It couldn't. Billy had snapped off its eye teeth to prevent it killing its prey. One day it had met a rat in a huge potato pile and unaware of the fact that his broken fangs made for an unequal contest, it had tackled the rat, which quickly slashed out the eye of the ferret.

Billy was the most totally amoral person I have ever met. If he wanted something he merely took it. When he was caught for burglary or poaching he steadfastly refused to pay the fine and worked off his punishment in " hard labour ". He never complained about his punishments. To him prison was an occupational hazard of the life he led. Nothing could deter him from the poaching, thieving way he lived. I was soon to realise why every game keeper and farmer hated Billy. Once he had gone too far for the long suffering pheasant rearers. He had raided a pen just before the young pheasants were due to be released. The keepers knew better than to try to bring a prosecution against Billy and had taken the law into their own hands. They waited for him one night and beat and kicked him until he was damned nigh dead. His ribs, jaw and shoulder blades were all fractured. " Why didn't you go to the police, Billy?" I asked. " What for?" sneered Billy, " 'twas a Bobby who was doing most of the kicking ".

Billy had not worked since he was seventeen. He had been apprenticed to a wood carver and he had a reputation for having considerable skill as a cabinet maker, but the 8 a.m.—6 p.m. life was not for Billy so he packed up the job and took to living on his wits. He had served sometime as a terrier man to a local hunt, but had fallen into disfavour when he was found selling foxes to a rival hunt. After his dismissal Billy had entered into an uneasy peace with the local hunting gentry. They knew Billy well enough to leave him alone even though he killed a fox or two each year. Billy was never one to forgive and live and let live. When someone hurt him, he had to repay the insult. When a keeper of a nearby river stretch had beaten up Billy for poaching trout, Billy had limed his brook and dead trout floated everywhere. When a farmer had peppered his lurcher with buckshot Billy burned down his rick. Everyone knew who was to blame for these felonies but proving it was another matter. In the end people learned to tolerate Billy's petty pilfering and poaching and knew better than to cross him just as a dog puts up with a certain number of fleas.

Every insult just had to be avenged. Once when we were sharing a railway embankment a fox had discovered the dead rabbit lying in the wires. All that remained of the rabbit was a bloodstained head. We inspected the snares and Billy with evil in his heart hissed "fox". He went to his dirty little workshop and took a fine sliver of jagged highly sprung steel. He bent the steel double and tied it in this position with a piece of dirty surgical cat gut—the sort that dissolves inside a person or animal. He then made fat balls from melted down putrid breast of mutton obtained from a fat ewe which had died in labour. To this molten fat he had stirred in an aromatic mixture that had hints of nepeta and aniseed in its make-up. Billy's mixture could draw foxes for miles. He pressed his "spring" into the fat ball. Foxes wolfed down this strangely scented fat. After a matter of an hour or so stomach juices of the fox dissolved the cat gut and the piece of metal sprung open slashing the stomach or intestine of the fox. I found several foxes and two dogs that had died in appalling agony from Billy's little invention. It is undoubtedly the very nastiest method of fox killing I know. It was certain that few floxes survived Billy's "genius". He seemed positively unmoved by the agonies of the animals he trapped.

Once Billy had been "set up", by the local gamekeepers, for a poaching charge he did not commit. Billy went to court, was offensive to an already unsympathetic magistrate and was given a huge fine. He openly stated that he had no intention of paying the fine and paid for his crime in "hard". His conduct in prison was exemplary—all he lived for was his revenge when he came out, and this time his revenge was curious. A week after he "came out" a large number of sitting pheasants had been literally slaughtered and their eggs smashed. Such wanton destruction was not like Billy's usual method. Normally he would have sold the slaughtered pheasants, these had been literally hacked to pieces. One evening Billy was seen casually wandering near Bland Pool carrying a full sack. Bland Pool was an old bottomless lime pit that had filled up with water and was deep, and murky enough to house a Kraken or a Loch Ness Monster. Three keepers came at Billy at once and he hurled the sack into the pool. A cry of jubilation came from Billy's mortal enemy, the headkeeper. Three keepers all ready to swear they had seen Billy hurl the sack into the pool and this time no need to perjure themselves. Billy spent the night in the local police station and next morning he was taken to the edge of the pool to watch three wet and cold keepers drag the bottom for the sack. Billy pleaded his innocence, but as the keepers said "They'd got him". Straight out of prison and on a poaching charge is well worth the maximum any magistrates court could sentence. After a day's paddling in the icy water they found the sack, but their jubilation changed to dismay when they opened it and found it filled with stones and rotten potatoes. They thumped Billy around a little and then released him. Inspite of his bruises he walked home laughing.

It is often said that people get like their dogs. In Billy's case the dogs grew up to be like him, for Billy encouraged this. Billy would never buy or accept a lurcher as a gift. He had to breed his own. He would negotiate for a greyhound bitch from a local flapping track, one that had been crippled or become too old for racing. Billy had no intention of paying out money for a greyhound, and he found little difficulty in having one " free to a good home ". Most of his bitches were near season and when they were ready to stand he would " borrow " one of the shepherd dogs that roamed the village. The collie would now disappear for ten or twelve days and only reappear when the greyhound bitch refused to stand for mating. As soon as the littler were born, Billy would bite off the tiny dewclaws with his teeth. He studied his litter daily making mental notes which was the first out of the box, which was the first to open its eyes and which made the first moves to suck the scraped rabbit kidneys Billy offered the litter. By three weeks old Billy had made his choice and he took his puppy away and reared it by feeding it scraped meat, milk and pulverised rabbit kidneys. The puppy was only allowed to feed from the palm of his hand and never allowed near to its brothers and sisters. Billy became its entire world. When he went out he carried the suckling puppy inside his shirt. He took it to bed with him, and allowed it to sleep on his sweat stained clothes. Small wonder the dog worshipped Billy. Many of the dogs were so besotted with Billy that they would bite through a door to get near him. I never saw Billy kick or beat his dogs, though he was never a kind sort of man. When the lurcher litter was weaned he took the greyhound bitch into the woods attracted her attention to a distant object and severed her spine with a sharp mattock burying her where she fell. Sentiment played no part in the highly complex make-up of Billy Robbins.

Billy's dogs were canine replicas of Billy (four legged, thieving, canine mirror-images almost). If dogs can be amoral Billy's dogs were. I remember one day I stood in Billy's backyard watching his nimble fingers working like lighting to make beautiful purse nets. His lurcher bitch, Moss suddenly leaped the gate carrying a dead piglet in her mouth. I thought she had found a corpse on the midden pile of a nearby farm, but when she dropped the " body " at Billy's feet, the corpse suddenly opened one eye.

Billy took out his briar handled pocket knife and slit the piglets throat, holding the tiny threshing body over the drain to allow it to bleed to death. Billy smiled and explained: The farm nearby bred many litters of pigs and Moss would crouch for hours on the pigsty walls waiting until the sows attention was diverted from the piglets. She would then leap down snatch up a piglet and make for home with her squealing prize to share it with Billy. Farmers undoubtedly noticed the loss, but probably put it down to cannibalism which is common among sows with litters. Once Moss returned home with a piglet but when Billy examined her, she had an immense gash in her side, I helped Billy stitch up the horrifying wound that had nearly exposed her intestine. The sow was a little quicker than Moss expected.

Just before the opening of the pheasant shooting season, Billy would kill quite a few. He used an old dodge with only a slight variation. He would thread raisins with thick horse hair, and leave them for the feeding pheasants. Pheasants would come running for these delicacies and wolf them down. When they tried to swallow the bait however it was a different matter for the coarse horse hair stuck in craws. The pheasants went literally frantic trying to shake out the raisins and in a day were exhausted wrecks. Billy stood near the feeding ground and sent in Moss. She promptly killed all the puzzled pheasants and retrieved them to hand. One day Billy sold over sixty pheasants he had taken with this method. Small wonder Moss was eventually shot by a keeper who sensed Moss would remove his means of a livelihood. Such a dog would be a curse on any game estate. The collie blood made the dog as full of guile as any beast alive, and the greyhound blood gave it just enough speed to make it a useful hunting dog. Few people have harnessed these attributes better than Billy did.

Billy was the ultimate in self sufficiency. If he wanted something he stole or poached it. If he could not steal the article he required he sold something else he had stolen to buy the goods he wanted. Billy made most of his trading transactions from the corner seat of the local pub. Moss curled herself into a tight ball under this seat. Sometime during the evening one of the local boys would come across to ask Billy if he would get a rabbit or hare for him. Billy would gaze at his glass and name a price—he would never waver from that price, no matter how much the purchaser would haggle. Once the buyer agreed, Billy would finish his half of bitter, cough, and wipe his mouth with the back of his hand give a quick " Yick " to Moss and be gone. I never once saw Billy let a customer down. I was always amazed when he managed to bring back a hare. Even in her youth I doubt if

Moss could have caught a hare, but in her later years she was hard put to catch a rabbit. Yet Billy frequently caught and sold hares. Once on one windy, dark night I asked Billy if I could go with him, and by now he had come to accept me enough to allow it. Outside the pub the cold of the night bit into me, but Billy and Moss were used to these late night ventures and seemed unaffected. We had walked about a mile, when Billy reached into the hollow tree, and produced a dirty yellow greaseproof bound bundle. From the package he took out a gate net and we walked on. At last we reached a field and Billy hung the gate net over the gate securing it at the bottom with stones. A strange fact about expert net men is that they seem to spend a very long time over placing nets. Billy was no exception. To place a gate net takes an amateur netter like myself about two minutes, Billy took at least ten. When he had finished Moss jumped the gate into the field and began to hunt like a beagle. Eventually the drumming of a hare could be heard, " Back ", hissed Billy and we crouched behind the hedge. Moss ran the hare around that field and it was never once in danger of being caught for the lurcher just did not have the turn of speed. Eventually the hare tired of the hunt which must have seemed like a game, and made for the gate. It hit the gate net and tangled in it. Moss, some twenty yards behind, loped up and hopped over the gate. Billy in spite of his rickety appearance was on the hare like lightning. Quick as a flash he grabbed the hare, and a rabbit punch silenced its screams. Within seconds we were heading back to the pub. The whole venture had taken less than an hour. Came unstuck one night said Billy " a bloody fox hit the net, and bit hell out of me before I realised it weren't a hare ".

Billy had never really followed regular employment, and made the pittance his wife demanded through the sale of illegally taken game. His big regret seemed to be that World War II came to an end when it did, and his mind frequently wandered back to the Halcyon days of meat rationing when keepers were called up for military service and the black out provided the ideal conditions for Bill's nocturnal way of life. " Glorious days them was ", said Billy. " Days when I could earn fifty quid a week just from selling rabbits and hares. During the days of meat rationing people used to line up to buy them. I used to get two shilling a piece for baby rooks. I cleaned up £20 one nesting time, and money was money in them days. Billy had somehow avoided conscription. He looked jaundiced and consumptive and the fact that he rarely washed made him look even more ill. How he fooled the army medical board I will never know, for his poaching trips and the effort of dodging keepers and police would have exhausted a decathlon athlete, but never as much as winded Billy.

I think I learned a lot from Billy. He was a source of fascinating poaching stories and a fund of natural history tales. Some of his ideas of how animals thought were barbaric however. If he was troubled by rats, he would trap one alive, dip it in near boiling tar and let the poor scalded beast back down the hole, " to warn the others ". Billy saw nothing wrong in the most inhuman cruelties. He was equally insensitive to his own ills which is strange for brutal people are invariably the first to squeal when hurt. One night I had invited a few friends over to my cottage for a party. My cottage was very isolated so late night rowdy parties bought no complaints from my neighbours. At 2.0 a.m. there was a knock on the door and I found a very wet and bedraggled Billy standing on my doorstep. He looked as grey as a corpse. Further more, his scruffy grease-stained jacket was slashed to pieces as if he had been on the losing end of a battle with a wildcat. " Christ, Bill ", I said, " what in hell has happened? " " Been shot up ", answered Billy pressing his grey face against the doorframe and nearly passing out. " Dig the pellets out of my back ", he hissed and then began to vomit until he nearly choked. My friends blanched and departed immediately. Billy's back resembled a close up of " no man's land at the battle of the Somme ". I cleaned it up and saw literally dozens of number five shot embedded under the skin. Billy had robbed a smallholding of some chickens and such like and been caught in the act. The owner had deliberately let him run forty yards and then fired. Billy would not go to the hospital as it would cause an enquiry into how the shooting happened and to go to the police would be beneath Billy's strange sense of pride. I am no doctor, and my biological dissecting kit had last seen service on a worm ridden dog fish. I began to clean the kit in methylated spirits I used for my stove. Billy took hold of the cup of spirits and drained it shuddering as he did so. " Heat the buggers in a fire to sterilise them ", he said, " I need the sodding meths ". I took my kit and probed about in the living flesh, but he never even murmured. When I finished I cleaned up his back in the iodine/ meths mixture I used for treating dogs with fox bites. Only then did Billy let out a hiss of pain and bit his lips until blood came ". " Billy ", I said, " for God's sake go to the police. No one has the right to do this to you no matter what you've done ". " You do what you have to do and I'll do what I shall do ", he said darkly, and I could not guess what grisly fate he had in store for the gun man.

Just a matter of a week or so later Billy was caught rustling sheep and selling carcasses to a wholesaler in the local town. He went to court and refused to pay the fine insisting on paying his debts in " hard ". One of the magistrates who fancied himself as being a bit of an amateur historian added that two hundred years ago such a crime warranted death, and Billy had fallen over in the dock in a bout of laughter. Such an outburst probably added two months to his sentence.

By this time I had obtained a promotion and with my mind set on higher things I had left Billy's sleepy village for the grimy town of Walsall. It was a mistake. Promotion didn't bring happiness. When I sit in boringly ridiculous and pointless staff meetings and remember Billy, totally wild, free and answerable to no one, I wonder whether in Biblical times Jacob avariciously counting his money in his tent must not have looked wistfully at the hills and wondered whether Esau hadn't had the better of the bargain.

CHAPTER 5

The Con Men

When I came to Lichfield I had no job, Lichfield held no magic for me and I decided to settle there only because I was able to buy a cheap isolated cottage with an acre of land. I use the word cottage with my tongue in my cheek for the property was little more than a tin shed. It was sufficient for my simple needs however and the land more than adequate for my terrier pack and greyhound. This was during the days when teaching jobs were a dime a dozen and I knew I'd have no problem in obtaining employment in the Midlands.

I spent the August holidays in my rat ridden hovel and explored the area. Foxes, rabbits and hares were fairly plentiful and though the land was let to shoots there were no keepers. A germ of an idea entered my head but it was so outlandish that I drove it in to my subconcious where it stayed like a caged hawk ever ready to fly. They were Halcyon days. The weather was warm and the corn ready to be cut and the vegetation hid the ugliness of my shed. I drew water from my well, boiled it for tea and coffee and lazed in the sun, but I was aware that such an idyllic existence would not last. Summer was running out and so was my money.

I knew that I'd have to apply for a job sooner or later, so I wrote to a nearby school for an interview. September came and I was asked to the school. It was a warm clear day and I felt good but it was a feeling that was not to last. My would-be head was a woman—a gaunt harridan who emasculted a man with a glance and would have made Hercules think that in spite of his "labours" he was inadequate.

She cast an eye over my clothes—I thought them casual she obviously considered them scruffy. The head eyed me as would a shepherd a wolf. After staring at me for a minute and studying my application for ten, she asked her only question of the interview —did I have a suit? I lied and said I did. The job was mine. Deep in my subconscious I heard my very soul groan. Life with this shrewish woman who regarded sartorial elegance as being the be and end all would be hell. On the way to the gate my schizoid mind fought a battle with itself. The secure side echoed my mothers warning (forged in the fires of the 1931 depression) " A man without a job is nothing " but my true self screamed out Thoreau's quote " A man is rich in proportion to the number of things he can do without " I had my cottage, had my dogs, land, enough for vegetables and I was living in an area thick with game. I needed very little. I tossed a coin. It came down Thoreau. Slowly I retraced my steps to the head's study to say I didn't want the job and that I intended to live off the land. She stood up and blinked, said something about my being a wasted academic and bade me to go. Thus began the most interesting and exciting eighteen months of my life.

It was once quite easy to live off the English countryside. The Anglo-Saxons found very little difficulty in the year that proceded the reaping of their first crop. There were hare, rabbit, deer, boar and even when they were really pushed for meat the flesh of bear to carry them through the bad times. The Vikings once called England the land of the fat serf, but that was long ago. My ability to survive had been put to the test during the freezing nightmare of 1962, but now at the age of thirty I felt far more able to make a go of my " noble savage " existence. It is still possible to live off the English countryside though if you are in any way squeamish, fond of exotic food or keen on observing dietary laws of Leviticus Chapter 11, then you had better forget living off the land. It is essential that one should be able to say " everything is edible "— and what is more, mean it.

It was Autumn. I spent my sixty pounds wisely and carefully and bought new rabbit nets. I rummaged around the local tip for lengths of copper or brass wire to use as snares and threaded it round the eyelets of old boots. They weren't as attractive as factory made snares but they worked just as well. I harvested the potatoes the previous occupant of my shed had reluctantly left behind and stored them. Autumn is an easy time for the man who intends to be self sufficient. Providing you are fairly certain of your fungi, edible toadstools abound at this time of the year and are free for the taking. Furthermore farmers who saw me taking ink caps and blewitts from their fields ignored me as they considered I was quite simply a lunatic. Any person who doesn't draw his dole and tries to be self sufficient is usually regarded as a bit of a nut anyway. Once I had to go into town on a bus to see my solicitor about the deeds of my property. I had put on my only decent clothes and must have looked moderately civilised.

On the way back I began to talk to some man who was sitting next to me on the bus. I told him the district in which I lived and he was startled. " I'd be afraid to live near that crazy bugger who has those dogs and ferrets and things " he said. He left me aware that I was that " crazy bugger ".

Rabbits were fairly plentiful and not only was I able to catch one a day for myself but I was able to sell the surplus to old people in the village. Whittington is a dormitory town and the younger dwellers usually commute between the village and Birmingham each day. These people will not usually touch rabbits, but the older villagers did. I sold most skinned, as I had a market for the pelts—it was only a few pence a piece but as I had no income at all a few pence was not to be sniffed at. One couple refused to buy rabbits skinned. They were of Polish origin and during the war years had been forced to eat cats. They were therefore more than a little suspicious of a skinned carcase.

I also had a fairly steady market for my rabbits in a village not far from my own. Here a German doctor bought about three a week for his siamese cats. He wanted the rabbits, skinned and gutted, but the kidneys left in. I realised why fairly quickly. The kidneys of a rabbit are similarly placed to the kidneys of a man— the left higher than the right. The kidneys of a carnivore like a cat are level. There is nothing as suspicious as people. By selling these rabbits I was able to get money to buy things like tea that doesn't grow well in Britain.

My dogs cost nothing to keep. I found a poulterer in Lichfield who gave me all the heads and bowels of hens I needed, and my terrier puppies sold quite well. I was quite amazed at how little I required to stay alive. My six hens, ex-battery and costing ten pence at Lichfield Market, layed regularly, even into the winter and towards the end of Autumn. I had enough money to buy a kid goat. Things were good, I was not prosperous, but I was still alive. I lived primarily on hares, snared as they crossed the main road that ran across a huge farm that had been converted to market gardening. I had no need to trespass, I merely set my hangs on the road side at night and collected my hares in the morning. They were impossible to sell. No one wanted them, for hare meat is dark and strong and civilized man is accustomed to bland tasting flesh. Subsequently I ate them. Most gourmets hang hares until, as they believe it, the taste improves. I was no gourmet and I ate them fresh. Cats frequently became tangled in my snares and quickly strangled to death. I fed these to my ferrets, it was only later that I came to consider them edible.

One day one of my terriers put up a rabbit a few yards from the house and ran it down with only a little effort. As I saw the terrier chasing on their rabbit, my heart sank—only a rabbit with myxamatosis is slow enough for a terrier to catch. Myxamatosis had come to our village and I knew it was the end of my rabbit sales. For the first time I felt suddenly apprehensive about my future. I started poaching further afield and bought a £2.50 push bike and went out early in the morning to check my snares. I learned to appreciate road casualty rabbits and hares, for not only did they provide me with meat but they also indicated that the hedgerows along that particular stretch of road were worth snaring.

March is a tricky time of year for beasts and hunters alike. It is neither winter nor spring temperature wise and rodents, rabbits and hares are often as hard pushed to make a living as they were in mid-winter. At this particular time the grove adjoining my house harboured a colony of grey squirrels—attractive, quarrelsome little beasts as aggressive and game as a rat. March is the ideal time of year to trap these, as the acorns, hips and berries have usually just about gone by March. I borrowed a squirrel trap from a gamekeeper friend of mine, " salted " it with maize and caught numerous squirrels. Squirrels are very good eating and I defy anyone to tell the difference between the flesh of a squirrel and that of a baby rabbit. The problem is of course to get a squirrel out of the trap without having ones hands bitten to the bone. They are incredibly fast and bite harder than a rat, I used to tip them out and let my greyhound do the rest, but my God, they really did bite.

April came and the first of my ferrets kindled in the darkness of her whelping compartment. She kindled earlier than expected, and when I put in my hand to stroke the normally tame old jill, she struck at me like a rattlesnake. Well, I had ferrets enough to last another year now and all seemed well or perhaps all was not well, I was aware that I was becoming increasingly animal in my outlook towards life. My sense of hearing and smell had sharpened beyond belief, and I was losing the last shred of culture that separated man from beast. More frightening still I was becoming less aware of the awesome loneliness of the life I led—I had few friends, and I think I had reached the stage when I would be talking to the dogs, and expecting a reply. I had no family, and I became acutely aware that I needed human companionship.

One day I cycled up the lane to find a bright shiny new Fiat parked next to my cottage. A huge, fat, immaculately tailored man was walking alongside my cottage. I eyed him with suspicion. He looked like a planning permission executive and the district could be very touchy about selling dogs from unlicenced premises. Big illicit businesses pass unnoticed in most smart fashionable districts, but a litter of ferrets offered for sale brings an immediate enquiry as to whether the occupant was " running a business!" I suppose the moral of the story should be if you are going to do anything illegal, do it in a big way. I parked my bike and watched. He stood kicking his heels in the patient manner that indicated he was not going to go away. I approached him " Do you want anything " I asked cautiously. My visitor turned, he looked like a T.V. type bishop " Do you happen to sell ferrets " he asked ' Planning official ' flashed through my mind. He saw my suspicion " I'd like to buy a good jill " he said quickly—Now few planning officials are going to know a female ferret is called a jill, so my fears subsided. He eyed my goat grazing on its tether " Toggenburg " he asked. He was obviously not a planning official. Thus Mark Wibley, the most gentle and plausible of rogues entered my life.

Mark was sixty years old. He was a retired bank clerk who reached retirement age and decided to kick over the traces and live the way he had always wanted to. He was not an original, Paul Gaugin the artist had tried the same thing. Mark had no artistic leanings, he was interested in poaching. Somewhere he had heard I was called " The beastman of Huddlesford " and other unpleasant names and had sought me out to teach him the trade. His close associate was a fifty year old fitter called Ernie Phillips, a sort of an amateur hunter who owned a useful lurcher and a slightly crazy terrier called Reg. We formed the most peculiar trio that ever existed, and our escapades are still the talk of the district. Ernie was as strong as a bull, I had the " know how " about snaring and ferreting and Mark had the most glib tongue I've ever heard. The months that followed were to be the happiest in my life.

Some five years before Ernie had bought a Russell type terrier called Reg, he was reputed to be a cross between a pied Staffordshire Bull Terrier and a Lakeland Terrier bitch. He was hideous and a great clown. As a terrier he was useless as he was mute as a steel bar, but he had opened the door to the countryside for Ernie who was born in Small Heath, an industrial district of Birmingham, Ernie had become besotted with the countryside.

He had moved to a village near Tamworth and after studying
Exchange and Mart for months he had bought a lurcher puppy—
reputedly a deerhound/greyhound hybrid. It was not of course,
it was clearly the result of a mating between some street dog and
a greyhound bitch. Pedigrees don't matter when a dog is useful
and Cassie was—in spite of his appearance he was an excellent
all round day lurcher—a mite bit slow for hare hunting but as
good a rabbit and fox dog as I have ever seen.

Ernie had a van so our poaching adventures could now take
place further from home. Our first run yielded the best haul for
a days ferreting I have known since myxamatosis. About ten miles
from my cottage was a farm owned by the meanest man I ever met.
Not only was he mean, but he was a thoroughly unpleasant skin-
flint. One day Ernie's lurcher chased a rabbit through a hedge
on to the Scrooge's land. He was gaining on the rabbit with every
step he took but suddenly the bunny jerked and disappeared down
a hole. Within a few minutes Ernie stopped cursing his bad luck
for he realised he had found a bonanza. The banks along the ditch
were literally honeycombed with rabbit earths. All were in use
and even from the farms bedroom the ditch could not be seen.
Now the owner of this farm let the shoot to two village boys who
had acquired a few shot guns and had bought the shoot for quite
a high price—one snag however—Scrooge's would not let them
take more than a few rabbits every time they were out. If they
had a good day Scrooge confiscated the surplus, put them in his
own deep freeze, and sold the batch to a game shop in Birmingham. As a result of this the rabbits population flourished as the
youths were reluctant to take many rabbits to fill the miserly
farmers pockets.

When I arrived at the rear of the farm, I noticed Mark
was immaculately dressed and wondered how he intended to dig
for a ferret or a rabbit dressed like Beau Brummell or a sporting
squire supervising a partridge shoot. Ernie was quicker than I
was at assessing things. "If we are picked up, then he'll deny
he was with scruffy ruffians, and dressed like he is the police or
farmer would believe him. Furthermore if we have to dig, he
knows we wont ask him to help and ruin his clothes! Well we
set to and netted every hole Ernie's dog marked. After fifty holes
we had to block the others with twigs and we still have to leave
many holes uncovered. Ernie's dog had hung back quivering as
he watched me put my dark polecat jill to ground. It was late
April—too late to ferret as there were babies about, but against
all sporting laws we couldn't resist ferreting these vast earths. I
will never forget that day. Babies hopped through the nest followed

by adults who bolted into the nets and were held. Some exploded from the unnetted holes and Cassie coursed them and retrieved them quietly to Ernie. After ten rabbits had been caught I asked Mark to call a halt, but Mark was one of those people who never quit while winning. Against my better judgment we continued ferreting for a further three hours, and by that time we had fifty three rabbits. Alas, now for the crunch. Disposing of a few rabbits is easy. Villagers would take those, and even ten could be sold by visiting a pub or a lorry driver's cafe, but fifty three! A visit to the game shop would bring enquiries where we'd obtained the host and in a town as respectable as Lichfield, police action would follow. Mark was a poor digger, very bad at netting but a fund of very wonderous, slightly crooked ideas. Ernie and I were covered in sandy loam we had to dig to get at two rabbits that had been killed underground. Mark however still looked as though he had just walked out of Austin Reed's. We put the enormous pile of rabbits in the car, and drove up to the farm. Panic seized me—what in hells name was Mark doing. He brushed his clothes down and went to the farm door. The miser came to the door obviously curious about his immaculate visitor, " I understand you sell batches of game to a game shop" said Mark and before Scrooge had a chance to deny it, Mark went on " I seem to have taken a large number of rabbits on my shoot near Lichfield and taking them to Birmingham is such a burden. Would you care to make us an offer for say fifty rabbits?" Scrooge eyed him a moment and made him a very mean offer. Mark did not answer so Scrooge increased his bid. " Done " said Mark slapping his clients grimy paw with his own manicured hand. We unloaded the rabbits and left, feeling like Edgar Wallace's "Three Just Men ". No one but Mark would have the panache to pull off such an amazing " Con ".

Shortly after this, Ernie, who was a great " noser about " found yet another rabbit colony. Once Ernie had taken Cassie and Reg his ugly terrier out after fox cubs and Reg had gone to earth and killed the vixen, and a fox cub had bolted, tangled in the nets and thrown them off just a field away. The cub had been run by Cassie and taken just as it had been "lured" down a rabbit earth in a railway embankment. The embankment was under-mined with warren.s Ernie, excited by his discovery came racing over to my house. Now here we encounter a legal problem that should interest the potential poacher. There is no law of trespass on fields, etc., if one is merely walking across a field there is little the landowner can do except order you off. (If you are in pursuit of game, well, that is another matter.) One can be prosecuted for just trespassing on a railway however, and the area we were in today to hunt was overlooked by two houses inhabited by Railway Police. It was a ticklish situation to say the least. Again we reckoned without Marks amazing gift for bluffing, he obtained two railway workers overalls from somewhere, and aquired a pair of very wide shovels. While Ernie and Mark poked about at the slag under the track, I hid in the undergrowth ferreting the holes and holding Cassie. When trains passed, Ernie and Mark waved to them and the drivers waved back. On the third day we worked this rabbit infested embankment, I glanced up and saw to my horror two railway police walking up the track towards Ernie and Mark. This was it—the end. I had visions of being photographed with a number across my chest. Goodbye unblemished record, and all the chance of getting back into the teaching profession if things should go wrong. Never underestimate a person like Mark, however. I was prepared to make a run for it, and as I was quick on my feet I know I could have made it. Mark would easily have been caught, but in poaching " the devil take the hindmost ". Suddenly I saw Mark actually beckon the two policemen towards him. Mark picked up a handful of railway packing " Since they have used limestone instead of slag, the British Railway has gone down the drain, its cut price everything these days, we'll soon be just like the continent ". Mark then gave one of the most boring dissertations on railway packing material I have ever heard, even I, crouched in terror four yards away, was driven damned nigh mad by this boredom. The police desperately tried to get away from him, but Mark refused to stop talking, tapping the limestone with what must have been thought a geological hammer, but was actually a hammer I had just used to tap in pegs for a rabbit net. The police eventually parted, thanking God they didn't have to work with such a bore, while I crouched in the branches feeling the beginning of a nervous ulcer developing. During the time I knew Mark never once saw him panic. He lacked bush craft and hunting ability, but he really understood the complex make-up of human beings—a subject I've never really been able to master.

Mark was a city slicker at heart and saw nothing wrong with " milking " fellow townies who came out to the country district expecting to find the villagers munching " wortzels " and singing about barley and mallards.

In Mark's local, various town dwellers from Birmingham came to see how " simple country folk lived ". I never ever saw Mark buy a drink during the tourist season. He was a wonderful raconteur and could keep a whole bar thrilled with his tales of poaching, snaring and ferreting. I never once saw Mark lose his temper or swear. He preserved his dignity at all times, sometimes in the most desperate situations. Once we were hunting a field near Tamworth, Cassie had taken about three rabbits, and Ernie and I were content to go home. Mark however was keen to try his ferret. If ferrets can be insane, this one was barmy. It was utterly unpredictable. He was a huge polecat hob, who rushed in instantly and killed his rabbit before it could ever contemplate bolting. We always had to dig him out. He was a positive liability to any poaching expedition, and I hated taking the beast out. Mark allowed us to net a bank and then against both our wishes entered his hob. There was some bumping, some squealing and then silence as the hob made a meal out of the rabbit. Mark bent to the bolt hole and made a sucking sound. He could never resist a lecture on anything he did. " Ferrets are bright creatures. I don't think they believe the sound is the cry of a crippled rabbit. They merely come out to investigate the noise ". He was also out to open up on Hebbs concept of animal intelligence when the ferret did come out to investigate the noise and being as Marks face was now inside the hole, he latched on to Marks nose. I fell over rolling with laughter as Marks head emerged with his huge hob ferret hanging from his nose. " Get it off Ernie ", said Mark quietly ignoring me and my hilarity. Ernie eyed his predicament calmly "How Mark!" he said. We pinched the tail and feet— traditional ways of getting latched ferret off a hand. " He's tightening the grip " said Mark with just a hint of panic creeping into his calm. Ernie suggested Mark should go to Lichfield Infirmary, but the thought of sitting in a waiting room with a ferret hanging from his nose just didn't appeal to Mark. Mark was now losing a lot of blood and I suggested that Mark should twist the ferrets body so that the blood ran down its nostrils and the ferret was forced to release its grip. Mark thought the idea macabre, but better than Ernie's idea, which was that we should cut away the part of the nose the ferret was gripping, with a pen knife. Fortunately my idea worked.

I was extremely happy during the time I spent with this amiable pair but about a year later Ernie and I went to fetch Mark to go ferreting. It was a cold morning but we were surprised to find the curtains drawn in Mark's tiny retirement cottage. We knocked and joked as we waited. Marks wife came to the door tearfully and announced that Mark had died in the night. He had been warned of his approaching coronary by the doctor, but he had not heeded the advice. It seemed strange that our amiable giant was no longer with us. Ernie and I " broke up " after this. The catalyst that made our relationship hilarious had gone.

My happiness came to an abrupt end. Three of my bitches had Caesarian operations and I owed the vet a considerable sum of money. My Halcyon days were over. With a sad heart I returned to teaching.

. . . AND RUNNING DOGS

CHAPTER 6

Why a Lurcher?

To the unitiated and the tyro hunter, it must seem a bit of a mystery why breeders should go to the trouble of producing a lurcher for coursing. Surely a greyhound, saluki or whippet would be more adequate for any coursing task.

Greyhound, whippets, Salukis, Borzois and Afghan Hounds are the athletes of the canine world. They are the fastest of all dogs and can attain speeds up to forty miles an hour, easily fast enough to catch even the fastest hare. Why therefore should the lurcher breeder go to the trouble of crossing these marvels of speed with other breeds and so losing a degree of this fantastic speed.

There are many reasons why a lurcher is more suitable for coursing than a pure bred sight hound. Firstly, sight hounds, that is those hounds that hunt primarily by sight rather than scent, are notoriously stupid and intractible. The narrow skulls of these breeds do not allow room for a great deal of brain. Sight hounds are only capable of learning a limited amount, and respond to commands with an infuriating slowness. This is a most annoying trait and could land a poaching man in desperate trouble. To poach game with pure bred sight hounds, particularly Salukis and Afghans is to court disaster. What is needed by the artisan hunter is a dog with a great deal of speed, excellent turning ability, a good brain and instant obedience. The lurcher breeder is prepared to sacrifice some of the speed of the pure bred sight hound to acquire some of these properties.

Furthermore most sight hounds are extremely fast, but tire very rapidly. (Salukis are an exception to this rule as they have astounding stamina and will run all day). Most sight hounds lack the stamina of the dog required by poachers or by a hunter who supplements his living by hunting rabbits and hares. Greyhounds and whippets are bred to run short distances at great speeds and when required to make repeated runs at rabbits soon become exhausted. Now a lamper or a man who courses hares regularly requires a dog that can run great distances and after a moments rest be ready to run again. Many " lamp " men run a dog as much as twenty miles a night. No greyhound or whippet would be capable of this. A Saluki might if it wanted to. A good lurcher will.

One other quality to commend a lurcher in preference to a pure bred greyhound or whippet, is due to the phenomena known as hybrid vigour. When two pure bred animals of different breeds are mated together, the offspring are tougher, more hardy and frequently more sagacious than either parent. They also usually have greater resistance to disease and have an ability to withstand greater hardships.

Lurchers, to the Kennel Club fraternity, are mongrels, but they are carefully produced mongrels—the result of ameliorating sighthounds with other breeds to produce a superior coursing dog. Good lurchers are rarely the result of chance matings. They are dogs deliberately bred for the job of coursing.

CHAPTER 7

The Traditional Lurcher

I have entitled my book "Rogues and Running Dogs" for strangely the lurcher has for centuries been the associate of vagabonds and gypsies. The Oxford Dictionary fails to accurately define the origin of the word lurcher, but Drabble in his famous " Pedigree Unknown " attributes it to lurch—to steal, I have doubts about the origin of this word. My own opinion is that it derived from the French le chasseur—a hunter—probably a dog which hunted by scent as well as sight. In Medieval times the greyhound was known as the gaze hound, a dog which hunted almost solely by sight.

About the only early reference to the lurcher in existence is in the 'Boke of St. Albans' by the Abbess Juliana Berner who refers to the lurcher as the bastard or false greyhound. Curiously many gamekeepers refer to lurchers by this sobriquet though scarcely for the same reasons. These false greyhounds were without doubt the result of misalliances between greyhounds and local cur dogs. Sometimes the misalliance resembled a rather shaggy coated greyhound—hence Juliana Berners description bastard or false greyhound.

Drabble describes the ancient Norfolk lurcher as being a cross between the Smithfield Collie, that drove the cattle to market from Lincolnshire to Smithfield, and the greyhound. Quite simple, but here we have our first puzzle. What was a Smithfield Collie. Idstone, writing in 1873, states that distinct types of sheepdog existed only in Scotland and his illustrations show a dog very similar to the trial sheepdogs of today. England however he states had no pure breeds of sheepdog and each farmer using any available cur to herd sheep, providing it had the necessary herding talents. It is indeed these herding talents that gave the almost legendary hunting ability of these Norfolk lurchers. Herding is simply an adaptation of the hunting instinct—the shepherd dog lures the prey towards the pack leader (his master) and must always be slightly bewildered if not disappointed when the master does not kill them. Make no mistake about it herding is simply a sublimated form of hunting. The collie that fails to sublimate its natural instincts becomes a ferocious sheep killer and any farmer who has a rogue collie from a local village raiding his flocks is certainly in for trouble. It is common knowledge that any working collie makes a damnably bad pet if bored as its hunting cum herding instincts are suppressed and they come to regard human children as creatures to be herded.

The curs which made up the Norfolk lurcher were probably a mixed bunch and included all varieties of collie and God knows what in their make-up. They were required not merely to herd the cattle, but also guard the herds and flocks from predatory dogs and roughnecks which haunted the Norfolk/London trail. Drovers had a tremendous reputation for being aggressive, as a glance at early criminal records will reveal, and the saying fighting men usually have fighting dogs is usually true. It is obvious that one of the ancestors of the Norfolk was a greyhound, but make no mistake about it the other was not the timid herding sheepdog of today, but a brawling, fighting, herding cur.

At one time I have no doubt that true breeding strains of this type of lurcher were kept by various bands of gypsies who roamed the country. They certainly kept a pure strain of terrier as the Bedlington once called the Rothbury Forest Terrier, a dog of gypsy ancestry attests. Various observers of Romany life from Borrow to Orford vouch for the fact that gypsy camps had distinctive shaggy greyhound curs running about and living rough under the horse drawn caravans. The diary of gamekeeper William Graham, who, with education, would have been a great literary man, I am sure, mentions with some anxiety of the arrival of Romanies with their shaggy running dogs. Graham was worried because the cunning of the Romany peoples and the sagacity of the dogs was a formidable combination for any gamekeeper to tackle. As I read this diary I feel the note of despair still present after the hundred or so years that elapsed since it was written.

The origin of the gypsy strains is unknown and any cynologist worth his salt will admit that data concerning the gypsy camp lurcher is pure conjecture. Perhaps they were the result of greyhound types that appeared among the morass of dogs that haunt tinker sites. Maybe they were the result of deliberately crossing the gypsy dogs that came into this country with their owners with English greyhounds, thereby creating a breed that was both fast and sagacious. Several gypsy dog-experts think otherwise.

Throughout Europe and indeed Asia almost every gypsy camp has its greyhound type dog. Many are similar to the shaggy coated lurcher that appears in Captain Trapman's book "The Dog". In Hungary and Bulgaria I found a strain of gypsy lurcher that bred almost true to type. Perhaps this true breeding or relatively true breeding strain of dog entered our country with their nomadic owners. One highly romantic theory that they were the dogs of ancient Egypt, for the word gypsy is merely a corruption of the word Egyptian. Early anthropologists believed that gypsies were natives of Egypt who left the country when Cambyses the Magnificent ravaged the land and attribute the fortune telling of the Romany to a hangover from the seer priests of Bubastis. Attractive as this theory seems it is in no way true. It now seems more than likely that the gypsy of Romany people had their origin in Northern India and migrated to Europe through the Slavonic and Turkish countries. Several gypsy tribes still exist in Northern India. These too keep pariah cum greyhound dogs around their camps. Funnily enough they were despised by both Moslem and Hindu not just for their thieving, poaching ways, but because of their highly omnivorous eating habits. Cats, dogs and jackals are regarded as delicacies, as are foxes and badgers. Few animals are considered taboo by these interesting hill gypsies.

Moses Aaron Smith, a now settled Romany, tells amazing tales of the sagacity of these dogs, which he claims, during his father's time bred damn nigh as true as any Kennel Club Registered breed. Moses states that they were deliberately kept pure of other blood and free from greyhound introductions to maintain their sagacity and ability to survive. Moses often says that no Romany would beat or kick a running dog though most were reluctant to feed them as it made them lazy. They were required to keep themselves by hunting and also to provide the camp with rabbits, hares, pheasants and game and even domesticated fowl which strayed too far from the farm.

At one time we deliberately cultivated Moses, not for his likeable disposition, but for his stories of his youth and his father's youth, Moses is a taciturn person, who will rarely tell these strange Romany tales, and is reluctant to show any person the odd ways he has of snaring and trapping—he is undoubtedly the best man with snares I have ever met. My friends and I held weekly talkings on Thursday (I believe sophisticates call them soirees) and we drank a wierd concoction to loosen our already free tongues. We mixed a very cheap damson wine with a spirit made by a Polish gentleman who made the hell brew from grain potatoes and sulphuric acid. What the proofage of this liquor was I have no knowledge, though the police records might give some indication, as our Polish friend did six months for his distillation work. This spirit mixed with the sickly damson wine made an elixir which brought forth amazing tales. Mark Wibley, my now dead friend, once said he stopped drinking the stuff when he saw the corrosive effect it had on the wine glasses. After a few glasses of this Moses would begin to talk and when he was ready for a tale, the whole rowdy mob listened.

His tales were invariably those of his youth and his father's stories of the Romany camps. As I have stated, Moses believes that these running dogs were kept pure, being bred for sagacity and hunting qualities rather than a turn of speed. One of his tales will illustrate this point. At one time his father owned a rough coated greyhound like cur that hated children and revered Moses father. When money was tight in the family and hunting poor in the countryside his father would wander into town with his lurcher. At that time before the public health regulations, the meat was displayed on sheets of greaseproof paper on marble slabs outside the butcher's shop. Moses' father would pick up a piece and ask the price. When he was told he would answer, "Too much", and put the meat back leaving his scent on the paper. In the security of the caravan he would simply look at the dog who would race back into town snatch the piece of meat and return with it uneaten. Once Moses says he returned without the meat. "Been sold" said his father philosophically who knew his thieving hound would not let him down. Moses says that the dog would retrieve live hedgehogs to the camp held gingerly in its jaws. The story book gypsy bakes them alive in clay. Moses with his knowledge of the real Romany, scoffs at this "We are not anmials", he says, "We stabbed and gutted the beasts before baking". Anyway he went on, "If the intact hedgehog was baked, guts and gall bladder would burst spoiling the whole carcass. Nobody would eat flesh tainted with bitter green bile". Moses also states his people would not eat hedgehogs caught by the dogs during the summer months as he says that they were invariably pregnant, suckling or the males tasted bitter. I cannot help but think what an accurate biography of this man would reveal in terms of country wisdom.

These lurchers probably had a great deal of herding instinct in them. One of Moses tales can again illustrate the point. He says one of the kin bands of his grandfather people were wandering in Suffolk during summer. Food was hard to obtain and the people inhospitable to the peg selling women. Furthermore some bug (not myxamatosis) had wiped out the rabbit population. Things were very bad with the tribe. The children went without food and the young people began to pilfer food in the town and had savage beatings in the villages from shopkeepers and police. Things had come to a head so the band moved north to Swafham. If there had been an attack of fluke or perhaps another disease (Moses is vague about this) in the sheep and the farmers were hard put to burn the increasing pile of dead. There was fallen meat a plenty, but no Romany will eat dead and diseased stuff. Moses' relatives fed the dogs on the fallen ewes and lambs for two days, to settle the farmers' fears, while his tribe craftsmen made two-foot long hat pins in the camp fires. Farmers were idle and were only too keen to give the " filthy bastards " all the dead flesh their tribe could eat. It saved them work burying them. The lurchers would then cut out a healthy lamb from the flock and corner it as would a collie. The Romany would walk to the sheep and stroke its fur plunging the hat pin to the heart and stopping the blood by thumbing the tiny wound. The group would report another ewe dead with liver trouble and yet another carcass joined the " filthy gypo's " only this time a fresh ewe. Moses says that one of the same band were caught killing a sheep in a stream—herded in by dogs, the blood and waste washed away by water. The farmers beat the gypsy so badly he died on the way out of the district and they buried him quietly. He had never been registered and had died well beyond Somerset House. The tribe avoided the village again, Moses face grimaced as he told the story. They hated us for our ways—we despised the gorgio (farmers and countrymen) for their stupidity ".

What happened to these strains of lurcher is a bit in doubt. Moses says that the gypsy now runs around in heavy goods type vehicles selling scrap, not pegs, simples and charms, and men now lay cut price tarmac, rather than hunt and trap. " Even I am settled " says Moses with a hint of despair. " We are a dying race and our dogs passed into extinction with our culture—regard adverts for gypsy-bred dogs with mistrust—they are the same breeding as you can buy from the backyard of any council house district. The real old stuff passed away with the silent people ", says Moses.

I cast my mind back to his tales where gypsies had no rights as people yet dwelt as free as Hereward the Wake—Mo's people lived and died as they wished yet even during Moses time the peg making, lurcher hunting, pure blooded Romany was an anachronism. I read the harassed pages of William Graham and listened to Moses' tales of persecution by Gorgio, I have no doubt just as the Ape-like men of old were forced out by Cro Magnon man then so was the real hunting, snaring, trapping gypsy crushed beneath the concrete juggernaut of society. A new breed of poacher was to occur—the profit hunter.

CHAPTER 8

The Profit Hunters

"With us, it is strictly for shillings", said Tom, who had come off the 'labour' in mid-autumn and kept his family of wife and four children on rabbits poached from all around the district. Tom was what is called a 'lamper' or a hunter of game by a type ,of searchlight. (John Winch, my great friend and barrister, flinched when I asked for the penalties of getting caught taking game by use of artificial light.) Tom went on: "Any person making a living by catching rabbits full time would only last a day or so if they only hunted by daylight". The rabbits feed a foot out from the hedgerow and are back in a trice if the dog as much as moves. True, one can sometimes catch a fool sitting out, and the dog will get him, but to make it a profitable haul then it's just got to be the lamp. Tom was yet another candidate for Botany Bay, for his two lurchers made massive hauls throughout that winter.

Firstly, however, a description of a lurcherman's lamp seems on the cards. Basically, it consists of a motor bike battery attached with wire to a car spotlight or similar device. Every lurcherman has his own methods of constructing a lamp, and every lurcherman thinks his opposition's equipment poor. To Tom, who is a bit of a perfectionist, and would be more than willing to send half way across the world to obtain the correct type of beam, my own lamping equipment makes him shudder. His equipment is checked daily and kept in perfect order, just as a 1914-18 infantry-man kept his rifle and bayonet in just perfect condition. As Tom says: "With us, it is strictly for shillings".

Tom's life is mainly nocturnal, and to get advice from him is hard. Like some rabbit-hunting vampire, he sleeps by day and consultation and advice is given only between five p.m. and the hours of darkness. If I had recorded his advice it would have had the interference of the whirring sound of his battery charger, always charging up the last night's worn out battery. One noted lamper I know states that he can only sleep when he hears the whirring sound of a battery charger in his bedroom. Tom's first waking hours are spent topping up his batteries with distilled water and checking leads and connections for faults which may occur on the hunt.

At one time I put forward my theory that Tom hunted rabbits as a way of following his natural carnivorous hunting needs or perhaps as a way of expressing his rebellion against the State or State rules. He said little and smiled. Tom is a bright, artistic man, who gives much thought before he answers. No, he didn't see himself as a Robin Hood figure, stealing the rabbits to feed the poor, and he repeated his " it's just for shillings " adage. Still, I kept my theory that it was merely a strange, archaic rebellion against civilisation and society, and I think I proved I was right some months later. But that, as they say, is another story.

Tom confesses that he is strictly a rabbit hunter and avoids running hares like the plague. When a long-eared one comes into the beam he shuts off the lamp and calls the dogs to heel again. Tom, with his ice cold mind, says the reason is strictly financial. He finds hares difficult to sell, heavy to carry in quantity and, furthermore, the energy expended by a good lamping dog on running a hare is equal to the energy output expended on the taking of twelve or so rabbits. Rabbits are easily sold now that the myxamatosis panic is over and, at the time of writing, will fetch as much as fifty pence each. On Tom's reckoning, a hare is just not worth taking.

Tom's reason is perhaps coloured by an incident which occurred during his early lamping days. Normally small lurchers, twenty-two to twenty-three inch dogs, are the ideal size for the lamps, as they are fast but nimble enough to turn on a sixpence. Sometimes an exception to the rule occurs, however. Tom's first really commercial lamping dog was Slade, a big Saluki/Greyhound cross, purchased from Welshpool. He was fawn to brindle, had a hard coat and, considering he was half Saluki, the most intractable of dogs, he was extremely gentle and obedient. He would run for ever and, after a day's rest, be whining at the door as darkness fell. Slade was big, twenty-seven inches tall to be exact, but his turning ability would startle a pure-bred whippet. Tom paid a good price for Slade, but estimated that he had more than earned his keep within the first week of hunting. He carried Tom through the moonless nights of the approaching winter and Tom found that he had to find a " no questions asked " dealer to sell the numerous rabbits Slade killed. One day, however, Tom arrived

at my cottage in a silent state which bespeaks that something unpleasant had happened. I waited for Tom to tell me the tale and,
after a heel-kicking session that always precedes a tragedy, he
did.

It had been a black, windy night that night and rain came in
small gusts. A lampers dream, thought Tom, unaware of the
tragedy that awaited him. Rabbits in scores sat out far from the
hedges and Slade slew them silently and returned them to hand.
The next field yielded even greater booty and Tom was soon carrying a load of rabbits that literally weighed down his huge frame.
Then tragedy struck, a hare got in the beam light, and Tom, who
now curses his greed, ran Slade at him. There was no need to
do so, Tom had enough rabbits to replenish the stores of his " no
questions asked " dealer, but Slade went after it. He was tired,
his night had been hard and fruitful, but a hare in the beam was
a challenge and Slade picked up the gauntlet. He took off after
the hare like a bullet, using all his now waning energy. The hare
kinked in the beam but Tom kept Slade at him. Tom ran him
at the hare a long time—too long, for Slade suddenly gave up
and Tom knew something was wrong, for his lurcher was no
quitter. He came to a slithering, sliding halt, shuddered madly
and keeled over at Tom's feet. Tom dropped his rabbits and
carried the 60lb. dog back to the van parked, for obvious reasons,
a mile away. By morning, Slade had died. He had given Tom
all he had by the time the hare had got up, he had then tried to
give Tom just that little more. The spirit was willing but the
heart just gave out. He buried Slade and forgot the long-eared
hares on lamping nights. He had killed a valuable dog and, after
all, lamping was a question of shillings.

During the winter, Tom rested his lamping dogs during the
full moon and ran the hell out of them on dark nights. Several
nights he called at my cottage half frozen from hunting in sub-
zero temperatures, frequently wet and always muddy. He was a
big strong man who gave up contract work on slabbing to take
up his will 'o the wisp life. The energy expended during a hard
night's lamping would have earned him a fortune as a slabber yet
Tom never went back to the soul-destroying job of laying concrete
slabs. Lamping had entered his blood. His friend, who was also
a lamper, had gone to prison for grievous bodily harm some
months before. Tom stopped his car outside my cottage on one
windy night when willow branches were being ripped off by the
raging wind. Tom looked wistful. " It's now that he'll feel the
hell of being locked up ", said Tom, and we both knew what he
meant.

As a provider of rabbits for dubious traders, Tom's life was hard. His dogs lives were even harder. He fed them only the best, checked feet and bodies before he ate his own breakfast and kept their coats in the condition a mink breeder would have envied. Yet he ran them damn nigh to death on the windy, dark nights. He estimated that a hard-working lamping dog would last him only two seasons from the time he began work in earnest. To run forty to fifty rabbits each night and each run lasting a hundred yards at thirty miles an hour must have a devastating effect on a dogs constitution. Other qualities also shorten the working life of a dog for Tom. Tom, a man who is certainly not callous, refers to lurchers as running machines. If one malfunctions, he sells him. At one time he bought a really good, agile little dog called Jade. Jade was a result of crossing a bull terrier with a greyhound and mating one of the progeny to a whippet bitch. He was a marvel of agility, he would snatch a rabbit through barbed wire fences, running at top speed, and yet return unmarked. He was never a fast dog, as he was only twenty-one inches at the shoulder, but his agility was a legend. I saw him catch all manner of objects thrown at all angles and do double somersaults to catch a bouncing golf ball. I pitied the poor rabbit that Jade singled out in the beam. One day Tom delivered his rabbits to the dealer. The dealer eyed the rabbits and said: "Last lot were bruised badly". Tom said nothing, but thought much. Next day the dealer said: "This lot were a bit chopped as well". Tom sighed and went home. That night he took a last look at Jade and sold him. He had become hard-mouthed and was no longer suitable as a provider of saleable rabbits. The man who bought him used him to supply rabbits for his own family and called Tom a fool for selling such a marvel, but Tom merely shrugged his shoulders and said: "He doesn't have to sell the rabbits. With me, it's simply a cash transaction".

One of my favourite stories about Tom and his droll wit is that one day, when he was at my cottage, I autographed a book I had written on the Jack Russell to a very 'plum-in-the-mouth' lady, who thought it worth the trip to Lichfield for me to put my signature on her book. Tom sat and watched her with his 'silly bitch' look on his face. "How many acres do you have to hunt?" she said in a jolly tone. "Literally millions", said Tom quickly, and she left without ever understanding what he meant. Tom went where and when he pleased, and although her story of his poaching exploits would have horrified and fascinated her staff-room in the rather posh public school in which she taught, Tom refused to elaborate. To him, such people weren't worth the effort.

I learned much from Tom. He taught me the wrinkles of lamping and I taught him to stitch dangerous belly wounds, all too common on dogs that crash into barbed wire at night. It was a fair exchange, as I shall explain in my chapter about the training, or mis-training, of the lurchers I owned. I confessed my fears of getting caught out lamping but Tom said the chances were small. One feels naked in a field with a brilliant beam shining nearly half a mile and a dog chasing a rabbit in it but Tom, with quiet wisdom, calmed my fears and came out with a series of pearls of wisdom; lamping is quite safe if one examines human nature and uses one's common sense. Firstly, one needs four places to legally rabbit—north, south, east and west. It doesn't matter a damn whether there are rabbits on any of the land providing the owner is prepared to say that you have permission to hunt there. Few Panda car drivers will even report that you are taking permitted game with an illegal lamping device; few of them understand the law well enough anyway. Tom has had several brushes with anti-poaching police, who are a little put out by his apparently quite meek and mild attitude. " If you are stopped late at night, you merely say that you are on the way back from so and so's place, where you have permission to hunt ", Tom says. ' The police usually turn your car over, which must be expected if you are found on the way home at four o'clock in the morning. They normally view your lamp with curiosity—tell them it's to find your way after dark. Few will believe, but it is unlikely that you'll be picked up for owning a lamp ".

" Furthermore, few police are going to really investigate a beam in a field ", says Tom. " If they call in reinforcements to sort out a boy with a lamp then they look a bit silly with a sixteen year old lad arrested as a result of a raid by four Panda cars. No policeman will come out to investigate the lamper alone for he has no idea how many people there are behind the beam. Not many farmers are very keen to leave a warm bed to investigate a lamper in their fields either and, if one does, it's easy to dazzle them with a quick flash of the beam, to switch off and to disappear in the darkness made all the more intense through the dazzling of the lights. Also ", Tom went on, " few farmers who rent a shoot will want to chance their arm to preserve game they have already sold to the shoot who has rented the place.

" The time of danger ", said Tom, " is when one makes it back to the car ". A policeman, gamekeeper, etc., will usually try to find your vehicle and then wait for your return. This is the time when most lampers get caught. Few policemen chance dashing across muddy fields when all they have to do is wait by a parked vehicle. I know one north country lamper who was caught by the fact that as he tried to rev up his car the keeper anticipated this and let his car tyres down. One of Tom's friends was caught with an enormous haul of game birds and rabbits when he came back to his car.

The moral in the story is not to be lazy, but to park one's car miles from the place one intends to lamp and walk back to it, taking a devious route across fields. My first genuine lamping/ poaching trip nearly proved a disaster as a result of Tom's advice, for I have the worst sense of direction in the world. Morning found me muddy with four rabbits, two lurchers and hopelessly lost. Eventually I hid the rabbits and 'phoned the police, stating that I was completely lost as my van had broken down and I had tried to walk my two lurchers to the nearest town. They found my van but gave me some very funny looks. They knew what·had happened all right. Furthermore, my damnable sense of direction made me forget where I had left my four rabbits. Tom watched me tell this tale, kicking his heels as he does before he speaks. " Some people can get lost on the way to the lavatory ".

" One fairly certain way to get caught ", says Tom, " is to have a dog that gives tongue when on prey ". Tom views any terrier cross in a lurcher with suspicion, for it is a terrier's nature to give tongue. Bedlington crosses, by dint of the fact that Bedlington terriers were often used for fighting, are nearly always mute. A lamping dog that yaps is a real betrayer. Few farmers will leave a warm bed to see the cause of a beam of light which could be a courting couple's motor cycle, but a yapping dog is likely to have an electrifying effect even on the most lazy farmer, who imagines his stock to be in danger through a dog chasing them. For this reason, most ads. in ' Exchange and Mart ' stress ' silent ' in their appraisal of the dog's virtues. The causes of yapping are perhaps many. It might just be the dog's nature to give tongue while hunting. Beagles and scent hounds are notoriously noisy. I think a far more likely cause is what I am about to label the ' despair syndrome '. In my earlier books on training hunting dogs I have stressed the importance of early success in hunting. The dog must make a kill early in his career. The terrier which hunts rats with an older, successful terrier and experiences failure soon packs up and quits when he sees a rat that he knows his colleague is going to catch. Similarly, a ferret who experiences an early thrashing from a rat will quit rat hunting. Now, a lurcher taken out too young and run on rabbit is going to find its young muscles taxed to the full by the pursuit of the rapidly disappearing rabbit. Hence, it experiences a hint of despair and gives tongue. A yapper is born and the habit sticks. Tom tells a tale of such a dog that he thought would be the be all and end all of all lamping dogs. One day a travelling man came to Tom's house to sell him a dog. At first, Tom was not interested but on seeing the dog he changed his mind. Gwen resembled a small, pied deerhound. The price asked was ridiculously low and Tom took her on trust. She was a marvel with hares but a bit too big for the lamp—besides, a pied dog stands out like a sore thumb when hunting ground on which one has no permission —but she had such a turn of speed that it was worthwhile to perpetuate the blood-line. His brother had a whippet dog, big for a whippet and had strong feet—clearly it had mixed ancestry as most track whippets do. One day Tom's bitch produced six puppies sired by the whippet. They were a beautiful litter, as I remember treating their feet for puppy ecezma, for the bitch had allowed some of the foetal fluid to stain the fur and the feet had begun to blister slightly. One puppy stood out from the rest as a flier. Tom had at last bred his ideal dog. He was going to make about twenty two inches tall—Tom's ideal lamping dog size. At seven months he took him out at rabbit on a nearby aerodrome which had a large rabbit population—until Tom's rival lamper reduced them to nil. The puppy gave chase at a fool, who sat out nibbling the long grass around the runway. The rabbit flashed back to safety in the barbed wire filled hedgerow and the puppy pulled up with a halt and, fault of fault, it gave tongue. Sadly, it was a habit it did not forget easily. Whenever it chased it gave tongue. Tom took another look at his dream dog, shrugged his shoulders, and sold it. For the hunter with permission on the land it was no problem but for Tom, who made his living from his poaching exploits, this dog spelled certain arrest.

Another certain method of getting caught, according to Tom, is the use of a stock-worrying dog. Any man who owns such a dog owns a liability; a lamper who owns such a beast is in for a fairly certain 'magistrates court' next morning. Cows always crowd round a dog running a rabbit or hare on the beam and a dog should ignore them. All that will be heard is the thunder of hooves as the cows race after the dog in an aimless fashion. A dog who pays a bit more than just attention to sheep, however, is a liability to end all liabilities. Lurchers coursing a rabbit or hare through sheep will usually cause a stampede but a dog who who will put in the odd bite or so will cause such bleating and screaming that any farmer will leave his bed to investigate. A day lurcher needs to be stock-broken—a lamping lurcher needs to be doubly so.

Tom owes much of his success in the act of not getting caught to the obedience of his dogs. Many lurchermen only insist on their dogs coming back reasonably quickly. Tom insists on complete lie/stay obedience. For this reason he will not usually tolerate a dog with a great deal of Saluki blood in it, for they are amazingly disobedient. Collie crosses are ideal, says Tom. Tom has good reason for wanting obedience. One night, while hunting a farm a dozen or so miles from Lichfield he ran into a spot of trouble. One farmer, probably suffering from insomnia, had heard some commotion and had 'phoned for the police. The police knew what was going on from the description so they sent a solitary Panda car, as lampers are rarely violent and so usually come up with 'fair cop' or poaching equivalent words. Tom and his co-hunter shut off the beam and beckoned the dogs to lie. They heard both Panda car doors slam and heard the crunch of size ten shoes on the frosty ground. After watching a lamping beam, Tom realised how weak police torches were. The torches came nearer and nearer and Tom clamped his hands on his puppies' muzzles to stop them greeting the law as friends. He says that he could feel the cold sweat on his face as the policeman's trousers brushed against his lamp battery. It was his closest call, and even the boldest man would be a liar not to admit to a hint of fear.

Tom will lamp right up to a gamekeeper's garden or a farmer's yard. Unlike the poultry killers of the gypsy camp, his dogs are broken to feather. They refuse to touch pheasants and such like for Tom forces the lurchers to pay daily visits to his pen of bantams. "I'm strictly a rabbit man", says Tom "and gamekeepers are not daft. They soon learn lampers of my sort are not after their partridge, pheasants and what have you, and leave us alone. If we killed a bird or so it would be different. To them, rabbits are pests and, although I doubt if they welcome us, they usually don't cause us a great deal of trouble".

Tom's deeds of daring are kept on the ground by his ice-cold sanity; not so his rival, whom Tom avoids like a typhoid carrier. "He gets lampers a bad name", says Tom, "and furthermore, if he did all the things he mentions, he would shut his mouth about them. Only a lunatic would boast of such things". In addition to boasting of taking peafowl, turkeys (which are always locked up at night) and ordinary fowl, this fellow actually boasts that he lamps the grounds of a local prison. Tom winced when he was told this crazy tale but then, with a look like a rabbit—catching Confucius, he said: "Probably quite safe, though if he can get in under the wires with a lamp and a dog then the security guards would have egg on their faces if the idiot was brought to court. It would probably be hushed up and the fence resealed ". Tom's blasé attitude betrayed just a hint of anxiety. If the rabbits were as prolific as his friend said, why hadn't Tom tried it? " Best way of getting caught ", said Tom, " is to lamp with a bloody idiot ".

It is said that if you become a teacher, by your pupils you'll be taught and there is much truth in this. Tom came to me because of my reputation as an amateur vet. and, though I cursed him for rekindling my interest in lurchers, I have much to thank him for.

When I trained my first lamping lurcher, I noticed that I could not prevent the rabbits making it back to the hedge before my bitch made a kill. The bitch was faster than Tom's dog, so I went for advice. " Try rocking the lamp from side to side ", said Tom. " It throws the rabbit for just a second or so and gives the dogs the chance they need. If that fails and the dog is far enough away from the barbed wire (Tom dreads the wire), then switch off the lamp for just a second, the rabbit is baffled and the dog has a sporting chance to make a kill ". That night, my brindle puppy put up another rabbit mid-field. It took off confidently towards the hedgerow, thirty yards to go, and I remembered Tom's advice. I shut off my lamp, there was a slight thump and a squealing. My bitch had made her first kill. I took two more that night by rocking the lamp and set off home with my three rabbits, all that I needed to feed my Siamese cats and their kittens. It began to drizzle and I hastily climbed into my van, the lurcher huddled in the back, turned on the heater and was prepared to leave. I had all I wanted but suddenly I thought of Tom and Jade, who would weather the cold and damp and spend yet another six hours hunting all through that cold and nasty night. My cats would be fed, but, to Tom, it was a matter of shillings.

CHAPTER 9

The Greyhound

The starting point in the creation of any lurcher is of course the greyhound or greyhound type of dog (Saluki, Afghan, Deerhound). A description of the greyhound and a background to the breed is therefore necessary.

No breed has a longer and more interesting history than the greyhound. Most authorities agree that the breed originated in the Middle East. It is likely that desert tribes owned these dogs before Abraham kicked off the dust from Ur of the Chaldees. Khorsabad has carvings of dogs that could only be greyhounds carved on its ruined pillars and the Pharaoahs knew of this fleet animal and used it as a motif to decorate their flamboyant tombs. Even the Jews prized the fleetness of this dog—the Jews who disdained the dog, though Lazarus had much to thank the beast for, and Jezebel had not. Solomon, wisest of men, eulogises on the swiftness of the greyhound.

About 200 years before the coming of Christ a noisy aggressive race moved from their traditional home in Britain. These Celts had had contact with desert tribes of Northern Iran perhaps and a trade in dogs must have taken place. These Celts brought with them their own strains of greyhound huge hounds used for coursing and also as dogs of war. One tribe, the Belgae, who had crossed swords with Julius Caesar, came to Britain and probably brought the dogs to this country. The Celts, larger than life, had huge greyhounds or greyhound type of dogs. The dogs were certainly in Britain long before the Saxons arrived, from Germany.

Elfic, duke of Mercia, kept a large "kennel" of greyhounds and hunted both hare and deer with his dogs. Most of the Celtic tribes had a respect for hares as creatures that harboured the spirit of the Goddess Lugunda. Britain is the only country in the world where the legend of the werewolf is replaced by stories of were hares. The Saxons had no such beliefs and hunted both hare wolf and deer with their greyhounds.

The greyhound was owned by rich and poor alike, the rich to obtain sport and the poor as a provider of food. The Viking conquest was to alter that. Canute, tiring perhaps of his defeat by the seas, turned his attention to the land and imposed the first of the notorious Forest Laws Canute decreed " no mean person should own a greyhound and the greyhound became perhaps the first status symbol in Britain, Canute had a reason for this law. The land was filled with forest scrubs and marsh and harboured plentiful game. Peasants hunting this land with greyhounds would rapidly denude the land of game and so Canute with a rather prejudiced eye passed the first of the conservation laws. There were many such laws between Canute and Edward III reigns. Anyone who sat " below the salt " could not own a greyhound unless it was maimed by severing two toes on the front feet of the dog. Shakespeare in " The Tempest " refers to such a practice " stopping for overtopping "—for the lame greyhound was obviously robbed of its speed.

Two types of coat existed on the Medieval greyhound both rough and smooth coats were found in the same litter. John Caius whose work on dogs is both extensive and inaccurate mentions that smooth and rough greyhounds existed, the larger dogs to hunt deer and the smaller variety to run hare. Abbess Juliana Berner in her hunting and falconry epic ' The Boke of St. Albans ' describes her ideal greyhound but she makes no mention of coat in her rhyming description.

By the Elizabethan period the larger rough coated hounds had ceased to be known as greyhounds and were referred to as deerhounds. These deerhounds were later to be liberally admixed with wolfhounds blood to become the splendid Scottish Deerhound. It took another cross to standardise the coat of the smooth variety however. In the eighteenth century Lord Orford used the blood of ferocious fighting bulldogs to improve the guts or " bottom " as he called it in his greyhounds. Thus the tight coat of the bulldog became an integral part of the make-up of the greyhound and colours like brindle and pieds began to appear among coursing dogs. Orfords famous coursing bitch Czarina was probably 1/16 part bulldog, and soon bulldog blooded greyhounds became fashionable studs. Broken-coated greyhounds became a thing of the past. It is also fact that the ear carriage of the greyhound closely resembles that of the bulldog. Orford's cross was a hall mark in the breed. It altered and refined the greyhound.

The greyhound has always been used as a coursing animal but competitive coursing is comparatively recent. In 1776 a group of people who were interested in testing the ability of their greyhounds formed a coursing club at Swaffham and, who better to organise the formation of the club than that pillar of the greyhound breeders, Lord Orford. Orford seems to have few interests other than greyhounds and was truly dedicated to his sport. So successful was Orford's club that other clubs were formed at Ashdown Park and Malton and ultimately the famous Altcar club the most famous coursing greyhound club in the world.

The rules of competitive coursing are ancient and quite simple but the general public is quite ignorant about them. I once asked an anti-blood sport league representative about the Waterloo Cup which he professed he had seen. His account is that a pack of screaming (greyhounds are very silent) greyhounds chase one hare until they catch and rip it apart. He had obviously not seen a course meeting.

Basically (and I shall deliberately over simplify the rules) a coursing meet involves several pairs of dogs competing against each other. One dog wears a white collar and the other a red. Hares are driven towards the pair and when the hare is given the necessary start—sixty or eighty yards, the dogs are slipped. Points are awarded to the dog which contributes most to the course or capture of the hare; and the judge signals his decision by raising a red or white handkerchief. Winners are matched with winners until one ultimate champion emerges. If the reader would like to see competitive coursing I advise him to go now. It is soon going to be outlawed. Funnily enough it is the blood sport that attracts most public indignation. Yet only ten per cent of the hares are killed. A friend of mine wise cracked " The dogs have to be agile to dodge around the angry anti-blood sport protestors ". Public indignation towards coursing is growing rapidly, I do not see it outlasting the 1980's. I advise any anti-blood sport person to watch the relentless war of attrition that precedes a beagle catching a hare. Yet beagling has attracted far less attention from the anti-blood sport fraternity.

Dog racing is a comparatively recent sport. The sport caught on in 1926, but there were other contests involving a mechanical hare as early as 1876. It was not until the late 1920's that Britain literally went to the dogs however.

Basically there are two types of track: the licenced track that obeys the rules of the National Greyhound Racing Club to the letter and the flapping or unlicenced track. On the licenced track the dogs are kept on or near the stadium and are checked carefully by trainers to prevent any malpractice. On flapping tracks the dogs are kept at home by their owners and as Cole Porter says "Anything goes". Flapping tracks are the scenes of the most amazing chicanery and cheating and sadly the dogs usually suffer from this chicanery. The prizes for the winning dogs of dog racing are very small and money is made by the owners betting on their dogs. In order to get good odds for a particular race it is of couse essential that the bookmaker holds a particular dog in low regard. Subsequently the dog must have run very badly in the race preceding the one in question and it is the task of the owner/punter to ensure his dog runs very slowly in the odds creating race. Many flapping track dog trainers have this form of chicanery down to a fine art. There are many ways of ensuring a dog runs at a pace below his best. One of the easiest methods is to keep the dog thirsty for about twenty-four hours before the race and immediately prior to the race allow the dog to drink until it wants no more. The dog enters the race with its belly distended with water and curiously it does not run very well. Some trainers give the dog a massive meal before a race. This has a devastating effect on its performance. Some years ago I lived in a hovel near a flapping track in Yorkshire and saw some amazing ways of ensuring a dog runs badly. One noted rogue tied two of the dogs front toes together with plastic thread. The dog ran a very bad race and when an official examined the dog at the end of the race he found nothing. Friction from the cinders had worn away the thread and tiny pieces of thread were hidden by the track cinders. The odds against this dog were really tremendous next week and the dog unhindered by his foot restricting thread romped home. One day I talked to this shady character as he took his dog down for the race it was not intended to win. The dog had a distinct smell of some chemical. After a few moments I recognised the smell as ether. The dog had been given a decidedly large dose of ether and was very dopey. Ether has terrible after effects, so dreadful that Simpson discovered chloroform to replace ether as an anaesthetic. It was a tragedy to see this dog treated so. He was a magnificent animal and tried so hard to win. On a licenced track with a fair trainer he might have made the big time. As it was, he made the greyhound knackers yard before he was five years old. I felt as sorry for this dog as I feel for most flapping track greyhounds.

Most greyhounds are finished as racing dogs at the age of four or five. What happens to these dogs is worthy of comment. Some society tries desperately hard to find homes for greyhounds past their best. Many are put down. Occasionally a licenced track is so situated that it can place a reasonable number of dogs but some are simply destroyed. Flapping track dogs suffer a similar fate. In 1974, 4,968 racing greyhounds were registered. It is of course impossible to find homes for all these greyhounds. A few exceptional animals are used for breeding stock, but no book on greyhounds is prepared to mention that some retired greyhounds finish their life as meat meal fertilizer.

This problem of disposing of retired greyhounds makes it very easy for the lurcher breeders to obtain a greyhound. Most greyhound owners are only too keen to find even temporary homes for their retiring charges. Bitches near or in season are very easily obtained. When a bitch comes in season she developes a slight deposit of fat around her internal organs. This prevents the bitch giving her best and thus for twelve weeks (five weeks before and seven weeks after) few greyhound bitches are raced. Subsequently as an over-the-top bitch approaches season her owner is very keen to find her a permanent home. A friend of mine visited flapping tracks to obtain biches for lurcher breeding. Within a matter of a few weeks he was offered over twenty bitches. The lurcher breeder would be ill-advised to buy a greyhound when such a ready source of greyhounds are obtainable free of charge.

Greyhounds are the most fleet of dogs but they can hardly rank as the most intelligent. As a result of this lack of intelligence greyhounds are extremely difficult to train to the standard easily obtained by dogs of a non greyhound breed. True some greyhounds display what is called track intelligence—that is the ability to manoeuvre their position while running. Whether or not this can be classed as intelligence is debatable. Greyhounds are certainly not tractable however.

My own experiences with greyhounds have not been exactly favourable. At one time I took on dogs for training. Most were mistrained dogs ruined through over-indulgence or ill treatment. Many were terriers that had jibbed, i.e. failed to enter to fox, badger or even rat. For a short while I made a sketchy and very poor living training these failures, and at the risk of sounding boastful I had reasonable success. However, I had failures. I learned never to attempt to train a basenji or a chow chow and I learned not to expect too much from a geryhound. I was once offered a magnificent track greyhound. She was two years old and far from retiring. She came into my possession through a woman whose husband had left her with three children and five racing greyhounds. The woman was a harridan and literally bullied me into accepting the bitch. Sally was a large bluish brindle and was so beautifully built that she would have passed as a show greyhound. She had excellent feet, beautiful conformation and magnificent colouration. All she lacked was a brain, I took weeks to teach her obedience. When called she would sniff a nearby object, wag her tail and then leisurely trot back to me or passed me as the mood dictated. After a very long time she learned to retrieve, but she took so long that I contemplated buying a spiked collar from Germany (they are illegal in this country) to train the bitch. I wrote to Tom Evans of Blaengarw an expert on training retrieving dogs and he told me that such behaviour among greyhounds was fairly normal, but he added that he had seen greyhounds trained as puppies that made a reasonable level of obedience, but he added " don't expect the bitch to be an Alsatian or Spaniel ". I persisted and eventually achieved reasonable obedience. Reasonable for a greyhound that is.

After a few months one of my lurcher breeding friends suggested I coursed her. He had several coursing greyhounds that had learned to run "cunning". (A term used by lurcher men for dogs that do not make a mad dash at a hare, but learn to predict which way the hare will turn and thus catch the creature). Sally proved to be very fast, far faster than a hare. She would run up to one and then run straight past never bothering to snatch up the hare. Bob Berks of Pelsall says this is not uncommon. During one race the mechanical hare broke down and three dogs ran straight past and finished the race. Sally would have been one of these. She was a beautiful, fast, well bred animal but as a hunting dog she was utterly useless. When I left the district I found an old lady who constantly remarked on Sally's good looks and gave Sally to her. She settled in as a house pet and is still alive today. She was so stupid and lacked so much killing instinct that I should have been reluctant to give her away to a lurcher breeder.

John Benton of Birmingham is a most persistent and successful trainer of hunting dogs. He acquired two very beautiful greyhound puppies and reared and trained them from the time they were five weeks old. Cilla and Sally were certainly the best trained and obedient greyhounds I have ever seen. They would sit, lie, walk to heel, retrieve and perform other simple obedience tricks. They were never very enthusiastic about doing their tasks however. A collie exhibits a fervour when performing. Although Sally and Cilla performed the same actions they were totally indifferent as to whether they did as they were told or not. They obeyed most commands but did so slowly. John hunted them to rabbit for a season and achieved some success. They were, however, brainless by any standards. Both Sally and Cilla learned to "lamp" fairly well, however, though they continued to run rabbit well after the beam was shut off, a heinous fault in lurchers. Sally was decidedly wild when she became excited. Once when she was hunting a rabbit I saw Sally heading straight into a single strand of barbed wire, I shut off the beam and prayed. God didn't answer my prayers. Sally hit the wire with a sickening thud. Fortunately the wire was rusted and snapped as Sally's shoulders hurtled into the strand. She missed her rabbit and returned to me waggling her tail. At first I thought that a miracle had happened and she was unhurt. She ran a few more rabbits and it was only when I was kennelling her that I realised she had a nine inch long deep gash across her neck and shoulders.

Paul Beatie, insurance clerk, who escaped the rat race by becoming a deer stalker in Scotland owned a big, black track dog that was a demon in dragging down wounded deer. He performed this task as well as any deerhound could have done. Brett, his greyhound, killed an enormous number of fox for Paul. If he was bitten by the fox that he bowled, he savaged the fox nearly to pieces. Once Paul came on a stray-cur harassing a fawn. Brett ran the dog, a terrier mongrel, and killed it. He had run on the track for four seasons and served Paul for a further five. One day however he coursed a fox who headed for a rocky cliff, Brett hurtled over after the fox and broke his neck. Paul still works a son of Brett, bred from a lurcher bitch of unknown breeding. One day Brett, working in conjunction with his son, hunted with a crossbred Lakeland terrier who bolted fox for them. They killed eleven foxes that day which is good going by any standard. Brett had also learned to "run cunning" and took quite a few hares for Paul. In spite of running in the most arduous conditions over rock, ice and heather, Brett never had any foot trouble.

Quite a few coursing greyhound men have coursed fox with their dogs. An average sized greyhound finds little trouble in tackling fox. One noted coursing bitch took a fox (that was accidentally bolted) when the bitch was 60 days in whelp. She killed her fox, and whelped a normal healthy little one of which was runner-up in the Waterloo Cup. Greyhounds often "wed" with great eagerness to fox, and furthermore usually start to hunt fox and heavy quarry far younger than a similar sized lurcher. Greyhound entered properly to fox tackle their prey with great fury. I once watched a bitch greyhound take a savage mauling from a large, aggressive old boar badger that had been walled out by a hunt earth stopper. In spite of the injuries she sustained she was screaming with fury and had to be dragged away from the skirmish. Curiously the bitch was a track reject who showed no interest in running the mechanical hare. She was mated to a greyhound/deerhound lurcher 'and became the dam of some excellent lurchers, one of which took prizes at the Lambourne lurcher show. Although this bitch refused to run mechanical hare she became an excellent coursing bitch and learned to " run cunning ". She took over a hundred hare and fifty foxes before she was retired to breed.

Quite a few members of American coursing clubs use pure bred coursing greyhounds to hunt fox: both red fox and the smaller more arboreal grey fox. Many have taken coyote using a pair of coursing dogs though the country in which coyote live is probably very rough on the feet of pure bred greyhounds. Still the fact that many hunters hunt medium sized predators with greyhounds is proof that greyhounds are efficient coursing dogs.

As I have mentioned greyhounds for lurcher breeders are easily obtained. Many lurcher breeders will only use coursing greyhounds for as they believe that the hunting instinct is stronger in these than in the racing greyhound that is only required to run mechanical hares. Other breeders will use any greyhound available as they believe that it is only fifty years since greyhound racing began and the track dog still has a lot of hunting instinct. Many books state coursing greyhounds are heavier boned than track dogs, but many light boned greyhounds win at coursing meets. Frankly I agree with Jimmy Keeling, the Liverpool lurcher expert, who believes any greyhound is suitable for lurcher breeding. Track dogs are certainly more easily obtained.

The lurcher breeder should not be particularly worried about the size of greyhound he uses to breed his lurchers. The variation in any greyhound litter is quite great. One litter bred in Sheffield was run on until they were eighteen months old. One large male was twenty nine inches at the shoulder and the smallest bitch measuring only twenty three inches at the shoulder. The litter had been bred from a useful pied male measuring twenty seven inches and a black brindle bitch who was twenty six inches tall. It is unlikely that a big greyhound will breed taller lurchers than will a medium sized or small greyhound.

CHAPTER 10

The Collie Lurcher

" To my mind ", said Tom one evening " the ideal cross to produce the perfect lurcher just has to be the straight collie greyhound hybrid. Not only has it speed from its greyhound ancestor, but it has some of the brains and super stamina of the collie. Nearly all top grade working collies are as inbred as hell as are all greyhounds, so the crossbred is bound to have exceptional hybrid vigour. " Got to watch the collie used ", went on Tom pensively. " The rough or Lassie type collie is about a quarter Borzoi ", said Tom. " They cross in Borzois to increase the length of the head. Borzois are famed for their fragility and brainlessness. They are unsuitable for lurcher breeding. What is needed is one of the working collies from Scotland, Wales or the Fells ".

My thoughts harked back to my childhood in a Welsh mining valley to the sheep that leaped garden walls like woolly deer and to the lean, mean, scavenging collies that shepherded them. They lived a miserable life, sleeping rough in the village shop doorways and scrounging waste from dustbins. Few hill farmers heeded their creature comforts. The dogs lived rough and fed where they could. I remember one pair that fetched food from pig swill as an enraged English bull terrier, piggy eyes ablaze, danced just out of reach on an immense chain. One day the bull terrier's owner installed a new and longer chain and I found a dead collie near the swill bins next morning. Collies that were not hardy and tough died off quickly under these hard conditions. During summer holidays I worked on one of these hill farms for two brothers who were more interested in ale and fighting than agriculture. During this time I never saw a collie given meat in any form, and often found collies eating unburned ewe afterbirths and rotting flesh from dead sheep. Many caught rabbits and rats to supplement their fleshless diets. They were rarely fed, never inoculated, yet they survived—by some miracle I thought at the time.

Never underestimate the hunting instinct of the working collie. As I have mentioned herding is simply a loosely sublimated form of hunting where the collie drives the prey (the sheep) towards the pack leader (the shepherd). One of my favourite stories concerned with hunting instinct, and indeed the sagacity of the working collie is one that is almost a legend in my mining valley. During the hard winter of 1948 every farm, except one, had a great number of ewes and lambs killed and eaten by a particularly savage sheep worrier. The hill farmers shot dozens of innocent wandering mongrels, which were foolish enough to stray out of the village. Nearly every large dog fell suspect, and many were put down to placate the wrath of local farmers, for every dog owner probably had race memories of times when the destruction of sheep merited the death of dog and man. Towards the end of the 1947-1948 winter when the hawthorn bushes on the sides of the hills were almost covered by the great depth of snow, one of the farmers shot a collie from a nearby farm in the very act of killing a ewe foundering in the deep snow. Sheep worrying stopped forthwith. Curiously no sheep from the collie owner's farm had been worried, but every other farm in the valley had lost sheep to the killer collie.

Matt Prichard, a curious type of Midlander, uses collies to lamp rabbits and has some large hauls to his credit. Though his collies are not nearly fast enough to take hare even on a lamp, they make large catches of rabbit. Matt's collies are particularly good at taking squatters or rabbits that crouch in the beam hoping to be unnoticed except that eyes shine like rubies in the darkness. Many good lurchers will pass over squatters, but Matt's dogs pick them up well in the beam. Matt's collies are rugged, skinny little dogs purchased from a working collie pair from Merthyr in Glamorgan. Both look more at home in a shepherding contest than in the hunting field. Many local lurcher men have mated greyhounds to these collies and bred some interesting and useful lurchers.

The collie lurcher used to be the most popular cross in the days when cunning was rated as an important attribute of the lurcher. Collies have cunning a plenty. Some years ago when I made a living from snaring and trapping rabbits I found I lost many rabbits from my snares. At first I thought that a fox had stolen my rabbits, but one snowy day I found dog tracks around my snares. Every few days I would notice a black and white collie watching me placing snares. It was obviously the culprit. It made a mistake however and one day I found it choked to death as a result of one of my snares. I took the collie back to its owner and explained how he had died. His owner, a very reasonable old lady, burst into tears and said the dog was a remarkable rabbit catcher but always brought beheaded rabbits home. I did not enlighten her as to why.

The intending lurcher breeder should not sell the gentle working collie short for courage either. Many will fight valiantly against any dog that invades their territory. Bill Brockley, the noted Derbyshire terrier man, once saw his shepherd dog, Mack, thrash a bull terrier that had come to the farm. Collies were once the bane of my life when I worked a delivery round on the hill farms of my village. Most regard any visitor as an enemy fit to attack. Furthermore not only did they attack me, but when I managed to get in a really damaging kick, they came back at me with redoubled fervour. I learned to freeze when attacked and escaped some potentially savage maulings that way. I remember one hellish day when a collie from Foch Wen pinned me against a hedge for two hours in the pouring rain and only allowed me to escape when it saw a new victim walking up the lane. Once while hunting in Merioneth I saw two slender hill collies attack and worry a big dog fox to death in a running fight which must have continued for over a mile. Both the collies were badly bitten and continued to worry the fox long after it was dead.

It was inevitable that show breeders should run many strains of the Scottish hill collies. To increase the length and profuseness of the all ready adequate coat and to breed in a long elegant head, the show breeder crossed the collie with the fragile and incredibly stupid Borzoi. True, an elegant attractive dog was created, a dog that fetched high prices as a pet, but as a result of using Borzoi blood, the brains, sagacity, stamina and hardiness of the Scottish Collie were lot forever. For this reason few lurcher breeders cross the elegant show collie with a greyhound in order to produce a lurcher.

I have no doubt this collie/greyhound hybrid produced some of the earliest types of lurcher. Many old books including Chapman's dissertation on working dogs describes the typical countryman's lurcher as being a greyhound ameliorated with some rough coated type of terrier, but I believe the collie or herding type dog provided the most suitable and easily obtained blood to bring about the most suitable lurcher for the artisan hunter. " Confessions of a Poacher " edited by Geoff Worrall states that lurcher of the latter part of the 19th Century was a hybrid between a collie and a greyhound and this cross provided the ideal combination of stamina, brains, courage and speed essential for the companion and helper dog of the professional poacher. Such dogs were not only required to take rabbits and hares, but were also required to assist the poacher by driving fur and feather into the long net.

One criticism of the collie greyhound cross is that though it usually has brains, stamina and hunting ability it is rarely fast enough for a coursing lurcher. Drabble in his " Pedigree Unknown " mentions this theory. Bodger Quimby, a noted Midland lurcher man, says that he has never seen a first cross greyhound collie that was fast enough to take hare. Thus, many lurcher breeders who specialise in breeding dogs for hare coursing mate the collie greyhound hybrid to a greyhound and the resulting cross being three-quarters greyhound is reckoned by many to be the ideal coursing dog, being strong, fleet and intelligent. As I have mentioned, the first and certainly the best lurcher I have ever owned was bred this way. Her sister was sold to a local poacher cum hunter and also proved to be a remarkable hare dog. She had a far more fiery disposition and would take fox or deer as well as hare. When she lost a hare she would cast about like a beagle until she found the trail and hunt and run the hare until she caught it. In her day she must have been one of the best hare hunting lurchers in Shropshire. When she lost her speed she was mated to a variety of lurchers and bred some useful if ugly offspring. Darkie Grainger, a wandering tinker who could shoe horses, weave cloth and trap almost any animal, bred some exceptional lurchers from the collie/greyhound to greyhound cross. The sire was a big broken coated black dog, a fierce guard as well as a superb hunter. Darkie allowed the sire to run free and it became the bane of every gamekeepers' life. Before he was four years old the dog had myriads of buckshot holes in his rough coat collected from the guns of gamekeepers who objected to the dog's thieving ways. John Masters, a schoolteacher in the East of England and an exceptional raconteur, tells me that the dog was not retired as a result of gamekepers' buckshot however. One day it had coursed a hare around a field that was being harrowed. The hare had dived under the harrow and the dog had plunged in after it. It retrieved the hare unhurt to Darkie. He ran and caught another hare a few minutes later and pawed its face as if in pain. Darkie examined the dog and found one eye had been gouged out as a result of the collision with the harrow. Darkie now retired him to stud and bred some excellent lurchers from him and a greyhound bitch that had been barred from the track through fighting. Some of these offspring made excellent hare, fox and deer dogs. One of these dogs actually supported his owner by catching a phenomenal number of rabbits on the lamp.

This dog is reputed to have taken 1,300 rabbits during the winter of 1973/74.

Joe Seggar, a noted Liverpool coursing man, is another fan of the collie greyhound cross. His lurcher bitch Lady is certainly one of the most intelligent lurchers I have seen. Lady is the progeny of a collie sire and greyhound dam and closely resembles a miniature deerhound. Lady was bought by Joe when she was two years old, and though she never learned to hunt with the lamp she was an excellent hare dog and had a turning ability that was hard to fault. Lady was also retired as a result of an accident. One day, while coursing a hare, she cleared a hedge and landed on top of some agricultural equipment. She returned to Joe very bedraggled and unhappy. When another hare was put up she refused to run it. It was only then that Joe realised that she had smashed a piece of the axis vertebra in her neck. Joe had only limited success in breeding from Lady. He disregarded the old maxim 'when breeding lurchers mate lurcher to greyhound' and mated the bitch to a collie bred lurcher. The resulting lurchers were certainly not what Joe wanted. Many resembled lightly-built working collies and lacked the turn of speed of either parent. Joe kept back one of these collie type puppies and states that though he was happy with the brain power of the dog it lacked the turn of speed Joe required. Joe sold this dog to a "lamping" man who found the dog admirable for the job, for lamp work calls for a particular brand of skill rather than a blind turn of speed. Still the axiom 'mate a lurcher to a greyhound' when one intends to bred a litter comes to mind.

In 1971 I spent the Christmas holidays bolting foxes for a colourful Yorkshire character called Jack Anson. It had been quite a hard winter and fox pelts were very thick. Jack had a market for wet fox pelts (pelts not pegged out to dry) and the furrier paid Jack three pounds for a good undamaged pelt. Jack had a pair of collie x greyhound x greyhound dogs, not good looking by any standards and not very good hare dogs. They were quick to learn, however, and mean as stoats. Both were lethal with any male dog they encountered, and so I had to use bitch terriers to bolt fox, and even my bitches brought an alert mean expression to their faces. The terrier I used was a rough coated tricolour bitch called Tuffy which would bay frantically at a fox, but never ever tackle and damage the mask or body of the fox. If we were quiet the fox would sneak out of one of the holes and slink away and high tail it into the distance. Neither lurcher had ever seen a fox before and they displayed only mild curiosity when one bolted. I was bitterly disappointed by their indifference and was prepared to take up my terrier and go home, when Tuffy marked a hole nearby. She entered the earth cautiously and gave tongue like thunder. It was a narrow, one holed earth and the fox could not bolt, subsequently we were forced to dig the fox. We dug the fox, a small vixen, and killed it quickly. Both lurchers sniffed the carcass carefully and one gingerly grabbed the tail and tried to pull off the dead fox. The next hole Tuffy marked also appeared to be a one holed sette or so I thought. I put in Tuffy and she rushed a badger round many times before Brock finally got through to the lurchers and convinced them of his fighting prowess. They kept clear of him in spite of the fact that Brock had only inflicted a few pincer like nips on their chests and necks. Henceforth whenever a grey one bolted they gave him a clear berth. No encouragement could ever persuade them to attack a grey one ever again. Some lurchers will attack Badger in preference to fox while others will not even contemplate a tangle with this the most formidable of British mammals.

Jimmy Keeling of Liverpool is also most enthusiastic about a certain collie lurcher he once encountered in North Wales. This lurcher was a result of a collie bitch mated to a large Saluki male. This bitch was a wonderful hare dog though because of her tiny working collie dam she was just a little small. She was however close to the high standard of perfection expected by Jimmy. This bitch was a wonder at predicting the jinking and turning of a running hare and could take most hares. When she was retired she was mated to a deerhound greyhound male and produced a number of useful progeny that made their names as coursing dogs in and about Liverpool. I own a grand-daughter of this useful bitch and she also retains much of the collie brains of her ancestor. Jimmy Keeling is of the opinion that this bitch might have been the dam of the perfect coursing lurcher if she had been mated to a good coursing greyhound.

There is little doubt that collie greyhound or collie Saluki hybrids make useful coursing dogs, but I should once more endorse Tom's advice to use a useful working collie rather than the elegant show collie to hybridise with a greyhound, and produce one's lurcher.

CHAPTER 11

The Saluki Lurcher

Since the 1940's there has been a growing interest in the exotic dog and one which has become reasonably popular in recent years is the Saluki. There is little doubt that the Saluki or at least the Saluki type is one of the oldest breeds in the world. Skeletons of this type of dog have been found in the tombs of Egyptian kings, and there are carvings depicting Saluki dogs coursing gazelle in ancient Assyria.

The Saluki or Saluki type exists in nearly all countries which were conquered or colonised by the Moslems. Traditionally all Moslems regard dogs as unclean but the Saluki is regarded as being different by the followers of the prophet. They treat the Saluki as an animal that is held in high regard. Saluki puppies are never sold and are given as gifts to V.I.P's from other tribes as token of respect for visiting dignitaries. Old women of the tribe are given the task of rearing puppies and of ensuring that the valuable bitches are not served by any of the numerous pariah dogs that hang around any middle eastern camp.

Not only is the Saluki a provider of meat but more important still the dogs are a source of entertainment for their sporting owners. Puppies of six months old are usually entered to the gerbil or desert rat by the boys of the tribe. Then rabbit and hare are coursed by the dogs. As soon as they have proved useful coursing dogs and proficient at taking small fry they are run at foxes, jackals and eventually the sable quarry—the gazelle.

Gazelle not only run at an incredible speed but they are also extremely wary and quickly race away as soon as danger threatens. This makes them very difficult to approach and damnably difficult to catch. To take this elusive quarry the Arabs resort to the use of the most unlikely and spectacular partnership. Arab falconers take nestling or eyass saker falcons or gos hawk at a very early age. The bird is fed on strips of meat hanging from the eye sockets of a stuffed gazell's head. The bird is never allowed to feed in any other circumstances and soon begins to think of the gazelle's head as a source of meat. The bird is now taken out and flown at a live gazelle. It stoops into the face and eyes of the gazelle in the hopes of obtaining the strips of meat. The gazelle is both blinded and bewildered by the ariel attack and often somersaults to throw off its attacker. The Saluki is now slipped and runs in and kills or holds the gazelle. This form of hunting (called Chirk hawking) is both ancient and spectacular. Most of the Salukis used for this form of hunting are of a different strain from those seen at most shows. The most commonly used strains have smooth coats with hair resembling the hair of an Arab horse. This smooth strain is apparently just as intractable as the more attractive show saluki which makes the feat of working dog and hawk all the more incredible.

The Saluki is a very relentless coursing dog. One day while I was in Syria the district was plagued with jackals—wild dogs twixt the size of the fox and the wolf. These dogs hid in the thickets by day and emerged at night to kill sheep and even newborn calves. One day some Bedu arrived. Sharp featured, tight skinned men unwashed and untamed, men of a tribe so ancient they had harried Moses on his way out of Egypt. They looked the very picture of freedom smelling of sweat and exuding pride and manhood. On their ornate silver adorned saddles they carried small lightly built cream Saluki bitches. Some young boys beat the thickets and the dogs were slipped on the escaping jackals. A pair of Salukis were slipped at one jackal and they bowled him several times slashing and tearing at him as they ran in. It was all over in a matter of minutes. All that remained was the foetid ferret-like smell of a frightened jackal. I looked at these arrogant young men who disdained to even answer my greeting and thought of the Arab proverb, " The cities make culture, but the desert makes men ".

Not only was the Saluki the coursing dog of the Middle East. He could also be a savage guard. Saladin, adversary of Richard the Lionheart, once laid seige to the Assassin castle of the Alamut. One night he awoke in his heavily guarded tent to find a hot cake under an Assassin dagger near his bed. Somehow the Assassins had got past the guard and the cake and the dagger were a warning that they could easily have killed Saladin. The Turkish lord cracked up and became a gibbering wreck. He reared two Saluki puppies and they never left his side, even tasting his food before he decided to eat. Guards could be bribed but a dog could not. Saladin and his guardian hounds then disappear from the pages of history.

The Saluki is intractable and this intractability prevents the Saluki from being the greatest coursing dog in the world. They are the most contrary of creatures. Many owners of Salukis become exasperated by their pets' failure to come when called and refusing to perform feats of obedience any street cur would perform with contemptuous ease. So common is this exasperation followed by rejection and abandonment of the dog that the Saluki club has a rescue service which tries to resettle many abandoned and unwanted Salukis.

Furthermore the Saluki has the reputation of being a habitual stock worrier and statistics tend to prove this reputation is justified Insurance companies which specialise in third party dog policies seem most reluctant to insure Salukis and their kin bloods Borzois and Afghan Hounds.

It could be the Arab is more tolerant than the Western hunter or maybe they are more sympatico with the Salukis' mental make-up and are therefore able to achieve better results with the breed. This may well be the case for the Arab values highly the sporting qualities of the Saluki and achieve remarkable results with this most intractable of dogs.

In Britain the Saluki is used more as show dog than a hunter though few Saluki owners can resist coursing their dogs from time to time. I have seen many first class show dogs kill hare and fox with considerable ease and know several reliable people who claim to have pulled down fallow deer with these fleet hounds of the desert. Salukis have remarkably good feet as they were bred for coursing over rough country, and subsequently rarely ever get their toes knocked up or their feet damaged even if run over very rough terrain. John Boutflower, a veterinary surgeon, was once the owner of one of the finest coursing Salukis in the country. This bitch was a smooth coated dog like the coursing dogs I had seen in Syria. This bitch was no more than 23 inches high but was an absolute wonder at coursing an amazing variety of quarry. She too was very disobedient and came back only when she was good and ready. She was however totally stock broken and would course a hare through sheep without even glancing at the terrified ewes racing away from her.

Jimmy Keeling, the noted Liverpool coursing expert, told me that he once hunted pure bred Salukis to hare. On favourable days and when the dogs were so inclined they did remarkably well at unravelling the twists and turns of the hare and were

capable of electrifying bursts of speed and that left lurchers standing. On other days they would course the hares in a most dis-
interested manner and even disdain to chase the hare. When on
form they were oustanding but they were so totally unreliable that
Jimmy forsook the breed and bred lurchers. Stories of this
unreliable side of Salukis are common. Keith Appleby, a biologist
friend of mine once reared a handsome gold and black bitch from
a puppy. She was a pathological killer, and had chickens, ducks
and a goat to her credit by the time she was eighteen months.
One day a fox passed in front of her and after a glassy stare she
coursed it. She struck the fox so hard that the sound of the
collision could be heard fifty yards away. When Keith arrived
at the scene she was dragging the carcass of the fox along a hedge.
She gave the mangled body a shake every few seconds to vent her
anger. When Keith tried to remove the body she attacked him
screaming with rage. Keith was delighted by this hunting instinct
and told a group of his friends in the staffroom of his school. One
day while he was golfing with some of his colleagues, the bitch
again saw a fox and totally ignored it.

Arthur Smith of Walsall, one time officer in the King's
African Rifles, is one of the few people who has had any success
in training this very intractable breed to any degree that
approached obedience. Arthur confesses that the dog caused him
considerable concern in its early training that for a few months
Arthur thought the dog was deaf. This dog would run most
quarry and unlike most sight hunting dogs he had an exceptional
nose and would hunt like a spaniel. Arthur, however, was most
enthusiastic about the dog's jumping ability and says that he never
found a hedge too high or wide for the dog to jump. John Holmes,
the noted dog trainer and author, is also most enthusiastic about
the dog's jumping prowess, and his book contains several pictures
of Salukis jumping what appear to be almost unjumpable obstacles.

It is not for jumping ability however that the breed is noted.
The Saluki possesses what must only be described as legendary
stamina. Drabble in his excellent book "Pedigree Unknown"
equates this stamina with the fact that many Salukis regard coursing as an exciting game and often refuse to "try" and thus never
take coursing as seriously as a really good lurcher might. John
Grant the taciturn and reserved Leicestershire lurcher breeder was
once given a recalcitrant and very savage Saluki by a neurotic
woman who had probably been normal before she had purchased
the dog. The dog had killed piglets, sheep, chickens and ducks.
It slew cats as a matter of course. It once hurled itself through
the windows of an antique shop because it had seen a tom cat

walking amongst the furniture. The dogs hunting instinct had
been choked by this kindly woman and she was very eager for
John to have the animal. John took weeks to break it to stock
and eventually took it out to course hare. It saw its first hare
sitting near a hedge and smashed through the thick hawthorn
hedge in pursuit of its quarry. John held his breath as the dog ran
the hare through an old gravel pit into a bramble patch and
through a flooded stream. The hare turned back to John and
died of heart failure a few yards from where it had originally
started. It was a Gargantuan run and most lurchers or greyhounds
would have been exhausted by it, but the Saluki coursed three
more hares that day and caught two of them. Hares were to be
the death of the dog. One day in January, John was poaching
some fields about ten miles from his home. Flame, his Saluki,
put up a hare that ran into a field in which a farmer was using a
muck spreader. In spite of the fact John was an intruder the
framer stopped to watch the course. As the Saluki closed with
the hare, the beast made one valiant desperate effort and dashed
under the muck spreader. The dog hit the spreader at maybe
thirty miles an hour and smashed its neck. John had bred several
lurchers from this dog and all had the sire's remarkable stamina.

As I have stated the Saluki is a fairly popular breed to use as
a base for breeding lurchers. Salukis have both speed and stamina,
and if another breed can be added to its make-up to make a more
tractable hybrid then the ideal lurcher may well be created. Saluki
greyhound hybrids are often offered for sale in " Exchange and
Mart ". Such a cross can be expected to produce offspring that
are very fleet and have great stamina, but it might be expected
that the lurcher resulting from this cross might be very intractable,
and bare in mind tractability is of prime importance if one is
using the dog for poaching. Some greyhound Saluki hybrids are
extremely intractable. However Tom Jones of Lichfield once had
a very tractable Saluki greyhound lurcher bred from a track greyhound bitch mated to a Saluki sire. This dog was most amenable
to discipline and became an excellent lamp dog retrieving game
gently to hand. Not every Saluki greyhound hybrid is the same
however. Some are very disobedient and difficult to train owing
to their Saluki ancestry.

A more popular and perhaps more suitable breed to cross
with a Saluki is the border collie. The progeny of this cross
frequently have the Saluki stamina but the Saluki brainlessness is
ameliorated with collie intelligence. John Grant bred an incredibly
useful and obedient bitch from such a mating using the Saluki sire
just mentioned and a working border collie bitch. Bella would

certainly deserve a place in the lurcher hall of fame. John showed me a somewhat blurred picture of Bella striking down a partridge which must have been seven feet off the ground. She was an incredible hare dog and earned John a lot of money in contests against tinkers who were foolish enough to bet that they had the best dog in the Midlands. Bella had a rough, spikey coat and stood twenty-five inches at the shoulder. She was so agile that she could charge full tilt at a hedge laced with barbed wire, and snatch a rabbit or hare about to get through the hedge and then emerge without having a scratch. As a lamp dog she must have been outstanding and killed over 200 rabbits in one noted week during a gusty December. I saw Bella pull down many roe deer going into a crashing rugby tackle attack and emerging without a bruise. One autumn day she had three roe deer over in a matter of an hour. She was very bad with cats and to John's despair would take off after farm cats with fervour. Cats were her un-doing. One day John was hunting a farm where he had permission. Many rabbits bred among the ricks and the trick was to catch one as it bolted between ricks. John turned the corner and urged in Bella. An old tabby tom cat, a fierce fighter and sire of half the local cats ran out and Bella ran him. John shouted until he was blue in the face for he had an inkling of the tragedy about to happen. Bella hit the tom hard and shook it by the throat until John heard the neck crunch. She went on shaking the cat long after it was dead. It was only then John realised that the tom cat had taken out both of Bella's eyes. He burst into tears as the dog tottered towards him totally blind. John led her home. He bred many litters from her and many were useful dogs but none were a patch on the dam. When God makes a super dog he breaks the mould so a replica is rarely come by.

Jimmy Keeling of Liverpool also talks of a collie Saluki hybrid in North Wales. She was bred from a small collie bitch mated to a medium-sized pedigree Saluki dog. This bitch was a wonderful hare dog and unlike John's bitch, she became the dam of many useful progeny.

Various other attempts have been made to incorporate the stamina and jumping ability of the Saluki with the qualities of other breeds to produce the perfect lurcher. I have recently seen the results of a bull terrier/Saluki mating which could well be awarded top marks for aggression and gameness, but were a shade too squat and heavy for hare hunting. A breeder near Barnsley breeds only deerhound/Saluki lurchers and swears by this mating for hare, rabbit, deer and fox. They looked very attractive and well shaped, but most looked just a little larger than the average deerhound/greyhound lurcher.

Not everyone likes the Saluki lurcher. George Martin who has bred many useful lurchers is decidedly unhappy about the using of Saluki blood in the creation of coursing lurchers. He believes that Saluki blood creates a dog that is invariably stupid and intractable. Like Drabble he believes Saluki lurchers rarely " try ". Still there are many coursing men who swear by lurchers who have the blood of this beautiful desert hound.

I will leave the subject of the Saluki and the Saluki hybrids with a curious theory put forward by my friend the gypsy sage, Moses Smith. Moses believes that gypsy lurchers were once a distinct breed, and came to this country with the gypsy and were not created from existing British breeds. I have certainly seen lurcher type dogs around gypsy camps in Hungary, so perhaps Moses could be right. As gypsies (the real Romanies) are reputed to have originated in Northern India it is likely that the gypsy passed through the native lands of the Saluki on their way to Britain. Could, therefore, the dog that gave the fleetness to the gypsy lurcher be the Saluki rather than the greyhound. Obviously no one will ever know, but like all Moses's ideas they have a hint of logic about them.

CHAPTER 12

The Deerhound Lurcher

Since the publication of Drabble's " Pedigree Unknown ", the deerhound lurcher has become one of the most commonly advertised crosses. The papers are literally filled with advertisements for deerhound/greyhound hybrids but ' caveat emptor '—,let the buyer beware. As the reader will see later, not all the vendors advertisements stay within the trades description act rules.

No more majestic dog than the Scottish deerhound exists. Even living in the most urban and squalid settings he resembles a ghost from a Celtic legend, a beast straight out of Tir Nan Og, a companion for a Cormac or a Lochinvar.

The Scottish Deerhound and the Irish Wolfhound share a common origin. It is unlikely that either were natives of Britain, being brought over to these islands by Celtic invaders. I find it not difficult to imagine these huge beasts accompanying their Celtic masters as they migrated from their homes in Southern Russia to pillage Greece, and wind their boisterous, colourful, musical way across Europe, finally invading and settling our islands. They were the dogs of those savage Pictish and Celtic chiefs who laughingly bit the noses from their captive rivals. Dogs so large and powerful that they were a match for the formidable grey wolves which roamed Britain prior to the Norman Conquest. Ireland boasted the finest of these hounds and the chieftains and nobles who kept them used them to hunt the enormous Irish Elk —six feet at the shoulder—as well as to slay wolves, which harassed both men and flocks. Chieftains alone owned these hounds and fought wars to get ownership of some of the famous dogs. Where else than in Ireland could a war be fought for the possession of a dog.

Arrian, the Roman cynologist and historian, says that the legions who fought against the invading Celtic hordes brought back stories of huge shaggy hounds fighting alongside their quarrelsome owners. Formidable dogs these hounds were. One famous story tells of such a hound who belonged to a crusty and belligerent chieftain called Culain. When the dog roamed inside the stockade which surrounded his house Culain was safe, for the hound was more than a match for any armed man. A youth called Setanta was required to take a message to Culain and climbed the stockade. He was immediately attacked by Culain's hound, but Setanta was the stuff of super heroes and, after a tremendous struggle, strangled the hound to death. Culain was mortified by the loss of the hound and was now in great danger of assassination by his enemies. Setanta offered to serve instead of the hound until a puppy could be trained to replace the old dog. Setanta disappears from Celtic legend and Cuhulain, the hound of Culain, as Setanta was known, goes on to be the most famous of the Irish warriors. Cuhulain, the hound of Culain, who lived his wild, boisterous, tumultuous life and who died tied to a pillar to prevent his severely wounded body from falling while the sons of enemy kings ringed about him, like jackals, snarling, but fearing to encounter him in combat, until a raven descended on his head and pecked out his eyes, proving him dead. No other race boasted such huge, larger than life heroes and no other race boasted such hounds.

When the Romans conquered Britain, the huge Celtic hounds fascinated them. Symmachus, the Roman consul, had several sent to Rome, where they fought both wild beasts and men. The Roman crowd, used as they were to the exotic, marvelled at the size and majesty of these ferocious ' dogs of war '.

In the year 1000, when Leif Erikson had pushed Viking influence to the shores of America, the famous Viking warrior Gunnar Jarl was sent a huge hound by the Irish king Myrkjarten, a dog so formidable that the Irish king said it was equal to two men in battle. These mighty dogs were great favourites among the Vikings, who took them back to their native Scandinavia, where many believe they became the ancestor of the boar hound, or Great Dane.

Time passed, and all that remained of the Irish Elk was fossilised horns and skulls dug up from peat bogs. Wolves became a creature long forgotten. Poverty and English rule reduced the noblest Irish king to a state of near serfdom and amidst such penury the giant hounds stuck out like an anachonistic sore thumb, and then they too began to pass into extinction.

A lighter strain of this Celtic hound became known as the Scottish deerhound. This breed, still formidable in spite of its diminished weight, was used to track down wounded red deer and hold them at bay. The Scottish deerhound still possessed the courage of the old Celtic hound, however. In 1760, a deerhound, aided by his shepherd master, slew a wolf in Glencoe. It was the last wolf in Britain. The killing of a wolf is a tremendous feat for any dog, particularly one who was only as heavy as a heavy coursing greyhound. Let not the reader dismiss the courage and fighting prowess of a wounded stag, either. A glance at the plagiarised epic ' Master of the Game ' will convince the reader of the fighting prowess of a cornered red deer. Not only must the working deerhound have great fleetness, strength and courage, but it must also have good strong feet in order to follow the deer across rock, bog and heather. Small wonder this dog, hybridised with the greyhound, produces some of the most useful coursing lurchers.

The greyhound/deerhound hybrid is popular on both sides of the Atlantic. In America the first cross is called a staghound —a curious name, as the American hunting authorities have decreed it illegal to hunt any antlered game with dogs. The reader should note that the British staghound is not related to the deerhound, but is merely an oversized foxhound. The deerhound/ greyhound hybrid is a most versatile animal. Puppies from this first cross are usually encouraged to start hunting rabbits. When they are useful rabbit-catching dogs and have developed sufficient stamina, they are entered to cottontail, a species of American hare that is both fast and tricky to hunt. When the puppies are able to snatch up cottontail and are well grown they are encouraged to run grey and red fox. They then proceed to formidable quarry, such as coyote and wolf. Gaston Phoebus, the famous continental hunter, says that nothing daunts a hound as much as hunting wolves for it is almost impossible to get a gazehound close enough to slip it at the wolf. Wolves are the most wary of animals and are rarely taken by surprise. John Allison, a noted American hunter, resorts to ingenuity in order to get the dogs close enough to slip at coyote and wolf. He carries his dogs in his heavily-sprung station wagon, adapted until it resembles a cross between a Land Rover and an estate car. (John usually hunts up to eight hounds.) When a coyote or wolf is seen, he drives across country until he is within two hundred yards of his quarry. He then presses a button that releases the rear doors of his truck. John says a pair of staghounds are usually more than a match for a coyote, but the whole eight hounds are needed to tackle a wolf. It is a frequent occurrence for his hounds to receive a savage mauling from a wolf. He has often had hounds that have died from wounds. Allison is a noted hunter who will only hunt hounds that he has bred. He uses an imported deerhound male, bred from a British Kennel Club champion, on to a coursing greyhound bitch. John is reluctant to use a track greyhound dam, as he is of the opinion that track dogs lack the fire of coursing hounds. Allison also refuses to breed from the hybrid lurchers. A few years ago he experimented with a litter bred from a wolfhound sire on to a track greyhound bitch, but he was decidedly unhappy about the results. Most would course the quarry readily enough, but they were far too heavy and ungainly to run the desert-loving coyote. Furthermore, they lacked the agility to catch quarry that are naturally extremely agile. Since this litter, John has bred only ' staghounds '. Allison insists that to get the best results from a puppy it must be entered firstly to rabbit, then to cottontail and, by gradual progression, to wolf. Dogs entered straight to large quarry are very easily discouraged when they receive a bad mauling from the coyote or wolf. Some years ago, John bred a litter which was bought by a vermin destroyer in the south of Mexico. In addition to coyote and wolf, this pack ran down and killed a fully-grown ocelot. Perhaps the deerhound helped tame The West. Marcia Frances of Gallatin, Montana, is the daughter of a pioneer who came to Montana in 1863. It was impossible for him to keep livestock in that area as wolves and coyotes created havoc with his stock. Her father imported a pack of deerhounds and wolfhounds from Britain and wiped out the problem predators.

In Australia, mongrelised deerhound/greyhound hybrids referred to as kangaroo hounds were, and still are, used to reduce the population of wallaby and kangaroos, which in desert or semi-desert conditions crop the grass so short that sheep cannot feed. In spite of their comical appearance, kangaroos are a tremendous adversary for dogs to tackle, and easily disembowel dogs with a kick from their back legs. Clearly, the deerhound/greyhound hybrids are the most versatile of dogs.

As I have stated, sundry mongrel lurchers are sold as deerhound/greyhound crosses to the unsuspecting buyer. Sometime ago Mark Wibley, a very reliable friend of mine, followed up every advert. for deerhound/greyhound hybrids. After fifty-three enquiries he found only one that was what it claimed to be. Most of the said deerhounds turned out to be rough-coated lurchers and one was a mongrel collie. The puppies sold would probably make excellent lurchers, but they would not be what the reader said they were. Joe Seggar, a noted Liverpool lurcher man, found great difficulty in obtaining a bona fide deerhound/greyhound male to establish a strain. He experienced the same problems that beset Mark. If you are buying a deerhound/greyhound hybrid, for goodness sake ask to see the deerhound sire. Deerhounds are becoming a rare breed, and few lurcher breeders own a pure deerhound stud.

As I have stated, many lurcher men swear by the deerhound/greyhound hybrid. Of the sight hounds, the deerhound is probably the most intelligent and has the best nose. In the progeny this intelligence is passed on, as is the incredible stamina and good feet of the deerhound. Joe Seggar of Liverpool had an incredibly good deerhound/greyhound lurcher purchased from Nuttall of Clitheroe, who breeds authentic deerhound/greyhound hybrids. Joe swears by the sagacity of this dog. Not only was Billy an excellent hare dog, but he was also a formidable guard. Billy once pulled down a half wild, savage pony that attacked Joe. As a lamp dog Billy was excellent. Joe and his brother were once laden down with hares that Billy took on the beam. Joe went to the Isle of Man once a year to run the smaller blue hare with Billy and he proved to be just as dextrous at catching this type of hare. Blue hares are not as bright or fast as the brown hare and in winter become a silvery white. Sometime ago, Joe brought several of these back from the Isle of Man and sold them to a Liverpool game merchant. Several old women refused to buy these as they believed they were tame rabbits. Billy eventually met his death as a result of a collision with a gate. He died of multiple spine and skull fractures.

Bodger Quimby, the most incredible and humourous character I have met in the Midlands, is also a fan of the deerhound/greyhound hybrid and states that no cross produces such versatile offspring. Bodger is one of the lamping fraternity and has taken huge hauls of rabbit and hare with his deerhound/greyhound bitch Bess. As Bess grew older, Bodger mated her to a pied track greyhound and bred a superb-looking bitch called Beauty. This bitch, in addition to being an outstanding lamp dog, is reputed by many to be the finest hare dog in the Midlands. Bodger made a point of trying Beauty against various lurchers in the Midlands and North and has done very well against all-comers. I own a half sister of this bitch (sired by another greyhound) and can vouch for the hunting instinct of this puppy. I took her out hunting with a few shooting friends when she was just ten weeks old. She was badly frightened by the noise of the first salvo, but soon settled down to the noise. She raced in and caught several rabbits crippled by the shooting party. Once she picked up a stunned rabbit and shook it. It came to and kicked the daylights out of the puppy, but she continued to shake the rabbit.

The crossing of the deerhound/greyhound hybrid with a greyhound is a very common way of producing a good quality lurcher. Many lurcher fans, Drabble included, believe this is the best method of producing the ideal lurcher. Bodger likes this mating as it not only reduces the size of the first generation dogs, but it also produces a more agile animal. This is borne out by the fact that Bodger's puppies jump like deer.

Ray Close, another excellent hunter and poacher, swears by this three-quarter greyhound/deerhound hybrid. Ray once obtained a useful deerhound/greyhound from Nuttall of Clitheroe. Sadie, as Ray called her, was a blue-grey, rough-coated bitch which measured twenty-seven inches at the shoulder. She served Ray well enough and took nearly three-hundred hares before Ray retired her. At that time fox pelts fetched £6 per piece and Ray and I did considerable fox hunting using my terriers and Sadie. She would kill fox with almost contemptuous ease and we took as many as four in a day with her. Funnily enough, she refused to look at badger and would turn and run to our car when one bolted. Sadie was as much at home in water as on land. Once, on one freezing day in Swinton, Yorkshire, I saw her swim across a flooded river after a moorhen, which had been winged by some thugs with air guns. The moorhen dived and fluttered to escape the swimming dog. Sadie eventually caught the moorhen before it reached the other bank, and retrieved it alive. She was also an incredibly agile dog and an incredible jumper, and often caught game birds in the air.

By the age of five, Sadie was ready for retirement. Ray hunted an old rubbish dump that housed a number of rabbits. The tip had many jagged protuberances on its surface and these played havoc with Sadie's feet as she raced across the tip at thirty miles an hour. She was invariably lame and her feet were terribly sliced up. Ray just had to retire her and, anxious to preserve the blood line, mated her to a large black track greyhound that had been barred from the local flapping track for fighting. I think it was the most ferocious greyhound I have ever encountered. Greyhounds are usually gentle with people but this one attacked man, cat or dog on sight. Ray bred some superb coursing dogs from this mating. Ray kept back a blue-brindle broken-coated dog called Garth and Garth concluded his bizarre life with a strange and macabre death, a fate nearly shared by Ray.

Rays' memories of Garth were bound to have been fond. Ray was a university-trained scientist who was engaged in metallurgy research. After a while he began to loathe the materialistic world of science and he opted out in the most peculiar way. He resigned his job, married a dress designer and went on his honeymoon in a second-hand hearse. Ray then bought a decrepit, crumbling cottage in the South of England. He began to live off the land by growing his own vegetables and fruit, supplementing his vegetables with fungi and berries. The cottage was in the heart of a game estate and when Ray bought Sadie it was obvious to all his friends that he was adding poaching to his country skills. Ray was the perfect example of the intellectual renegade. He was to become a thorough nuisance in his district and his wife stayed with him through some very bad times. I was going through a similar phase myself, and I was very much sympatico with his ideas. Ray regaled me with his amazing anecdotes and in return I taught him trapping and snaring. Lookng back, I think I had the better of the deal.

Ray's adventures with his three-quarter bred deerhound/greyhound were quite amazing and not a little hair-raising. As I have mentioned, Ray's cottage was in the middle of a heavily-keepered estate and the land held a considerable quantity of game. Ray, like Tom the profit hunter, was of the opinion that if a poacher gave the game birds a miss, few keepers would object to rabbits and hares being taken. The headkeeper, however, did not agree with Ray's theory. Ray lamped the land frequently and kept well away from the partridge, pheasant and roe deer the estate held but the headkeeper, a portly and officious man regarded any intrusion on the land as being an insult to his ability as a gamekeeper. If he had lived in Norman times, he would have had Ray and his fellow poachers hung from a gibbet alongside the stoats and weasels. He deliberately harassed Ray, accosting him in a noisy and offensive manner on the street and in pubs. Madelaine, Ray's long-suffering wife, said that Ray was treating the whole stupid business with a vendetta-like air of seriousness that was totally foreign to Ray's personality. Garth was the ideal poachers dog, quiet, obedient and wonderfully fast He never barked and never trusted a stranger to even stroke him.

As the shooting season progressed and various towny shooting men arrived with no hunting ability and a desire to slay every living creature on the estate, the keeper took to visiting Ray's house, as he mistook Ray's soft-spoken manner for timidity and believed he could frighten Ray off. He told Ray that he was in a position to put Ray away for a considerable time, and hinted darkly that he had sufficient power to get a court ruling to have Garth put to sleep. Ray sensed the obvious bluff and laughed in the keeper's face. For the next few weeks, Ray's van was checked over almost nightly by a local panda car driver but, as Ray says, that might have been pure coincidence. Another visit from the keeper followed, only this time threats and obscenities came fast and furious. Ray's patience snapped. If his keeper adversary wanted something to complain about then Ray would give him reason to complain. He consulted the game shop in the nearest town, the shop where he sold all his illegally taken rabbits and hares. Yes, they were prepared to take any pheasants and partridge Ray killed and, if Ray could get them, the shop would take any roe deer Ray might happen to get. Profit did not concern Ray any more. It was a matter of honour and revenge. His knowledge of poaching at this time consisted of how to breed good lurchers and how to hunt rabbit and hare on the lamp. He now frequented the lairs of old poachers who had done time for taking game. It was now full-scale war. He also contacted an elderly reprobate poacher whom the locals referred to as Deer-slayer. Ray was now ready to start his war against his keeper.

He began by parking his car at the opposite end of the estate he intended to hunt. With lamp and catapult he massacred the roosting pheasants, selling them for next to nothing to his 'no questions asked' game dealer. Although his haul of partridges was small, he hunted that estate so thoroughly that the partridge moved off the land to feed well outside the estate. He spread doped corn around the coverts and Garth took the 'groggy' birds easily. At the same time he hunted rabbits and hares almost nightly on the estate. Ray even took to going out on moonlight nights, the first sign that the poacher is getting cocky and is ready and ripe to be 'taken'.

Eventually, he was to have such a narrow escape that it taught him caution. One night while hunting a huge field, Ray, burdened with about twenty rabbits, heard a car motor on the other side of the hedge. He shut off his lamp and became invisible, but not for long. Suddenly the field became as if floodlit as a Land Rover came into the field, lights ablaze. Ray felt naked and froze. His adversary bore down on him rapidly. Ray whistled up Garth and ran like mad for the hedge. He had always been an excellent athlete and was very agile, but a Land Rover moves rapidly over muddy ground and, furthermore, it was obvious to Ray that the keeper intended to knock him down. Suddenly, Ray had a flash of inspiration. He vaulted the hedge as the Land Rover was nearly on him and Garth dived through a weakened portion of the hedge after him. The Land Rover was not as agile and crashed through the wire and hedge and finished up upside down in the ditch. Ray was in no mood to think about the game-keeper's well-being as he raced home and threw himself down, panting, on the hearth rug.

One of the curious things about poachers is that when they have had a very close call, they yearn to get back to the place where they were nearly caught. Ray was no exception and hunted the same fields within a day or so of his encounter with the keeper. Furthermore, flushed with Garth's success as a poacher, he mated Sadie to the black greyhound to produce another litter of the same calibre as Garth.

Shortly after this, the sands of time began to run out for Garth. Nights were becoming lighter as spring came along. One evening, a deer got up and, encouraged by Ray's cry, Garth had run it and 'had it over'. Ray ran in quickly and cut the throat of the screaming deer. Roe deer were fairly numerous on the estate and Ray had left them alone until this time. He was surprised at the ease with which Garth pulled down the deer, and from now on roe deer were fair game. Ray forsook the partridge and pheasant of the estate and hunted roe deer, which fetched £12 apiece from the game dealer, who did not ask too many questions.

One evening, Ray saw a large roebuck rubbing its antlers against a tree. It seemed oddly tame and unafraid as Ray and Garth walked towards it. Ray should have been warned by this peculiar behaviour. Normally deer took off as soon as Garth and Ray appeared and Garth ran them and held them, but as he raced at the buck it never moved and put his antlers down to meet the coming onslaught. The first collision brought a squeal of pain from Garth as one of the antler tines scooped out his left eye. To Ray's horror and amazement, the deer followed up the advantage by butting and mangling the side of the groggy and bleeding dog. Ray ran in screaming, but instead of running the deer lunged at Ray and a tine pierced his gut. Ray kicked and struggled to drive back the deer as he dragged the badly bleeding Garth to his van. What had caused this phenomenon was easily explained. The local grocer's daughter had found a fawn and reared the creature by hand. When he was sexually mature, he became so spiteful and vicious that the family were afraid of him. Things came to a head when a labrador belonging to the family was badly mangled by the buck. The family had turned him loose, hoping he could adapt. He had become the terror of the fields and it was Ray's bad luck he had encountered the beast. Garth fared worse than the labrador, for he died three days later from shock and septic poisoning. Ray was quite ill from his goring, and went into hospital for treatment. Garth's death finished Ray's living off the land. He returned to university, took a Ph.D., and went to America to do research. I heard from him a few months ago and he wistfully harks back to the old days when his rebellion against society so nearly paid off.

CHAPTER 13

The Bedlington Greyhound Lurcher

During the late 1800's most of the dog books describe the lurcher as being " the dog of the poacher and artisan hunter " or " dog of the gypsy camp ", and usually attribute its origin to a cross between the greyhound and a Bedlington terrier. Captain Trapman in his amusingly anthropomorphic book, " The Dog ", has an ink drawing of a very useful looking lurcher which he states is a result of Bedlington Greyhound hybridisation. There is little doubt that many lurchers today have Bedlington ancestry and the Bedlington greyhound cross was certainly very popular some twenty years ago. A glance at the ancestry of the Bedlington will certainly be of interest to the would-be lurcher breeder.

The Bedlington of old was indeed a hard-fighting rowdy and versatile dog. Story has it that the gypsy and itinerant tinker families, who lived outside the law in the wild district of Northumberland, kept versatile cur cum terrier type dogs. It was said of these tinker bred terriers with their soft linty coats that they looked like lambs and fought like lions. Rawdon Lee says that when two fought only one walked away from the battle. Not only were the dogs required to guard the camp site, but they were expected to be fast enough to catch a rabbit and game enough to tackle a fox, draw a badger and provide saleable otter skins. The gypsy families such as the Andersons, the Jeffersons and the colourful and noisy Faas also pitted their dogs against each other in " to the death " battles. During the horse fairs when these wild families met, men fought men in bare knuckle contests and terriers flought to the death. From the hotch potch of breeds that lived on the tinker sites a distinct type had began to emerge by about 1800, and was known as the Rothbury Forest Terrier.

At about this time a group of nailers from Staffordshire came to live in Bedlington bringing with them mongrel bull dogs used for dog fightng, badger drawing and bull baiting. These too entered into the make-up of the Rothbury Forest dog or Bedlington as it now became known, probably to make the terrier more suitable for the job of rat killing and pit fighting. From this morass

of breeds emerged the dog we know as the modern Bedlington
terrier. Stories of the courage are legion. Ainsley's Piper, as
game a dog as ever drew breath, once drove off a vicious old
English sow who was intent on attacking and probably eating a
young child left alone in a cornfield—a formidable task by any
standard.

Not only was the dog a demon with vermin of any sort, he
was also as versatile a dog as one could wish to meet. Few breeds
made such good guards (for many defended their tinker owners
with their lives during the horse fair brawls) but they were wonderfully at home in water. Many claim that this love of water was
due to the introduction of otter hound blood early in the breed's
history. This is claimed of most the northern terrier breeds but
there is little evidence to suggest that otter hound blood entered
into the make-up of the Bedlington. In the 1880's when obedience
type tests were becoming popular, a Bedlington called Nailor won
3rd prize in a contest involving rescuing a dummy from water. It
seems only fair to add that the first prize was won by a huge
Newfoundland-bred exclusively for work in water.

The Bedlington was ever a popular breed in mining villages,
and in districts where heavy industry produced a particular type
of sportsman who required a very hard dog. Many of the miners
of the South Welsh villages kept these dogs and used them for
badger digging and to their discredit, dog fighting. Some of the
miners in my own village mated Staffordshire bull terrier bitches
to Bedlingtons to produce a very hard working terrier. Such blood
entered into the Russell type dogs of that district which even today
breed specimens with fluffy top knots attesting their Bedlington
ancestry.

Tom Evans of Blaengarw, naturalist hunter and dog trainer,
was a great admirer of the courage of the Bedlington. During the
strikes and depression that haunted the 1920 mining folk, the
colliers often kept their digging hands in by hunting badgers in
the lower parts of the valley. Badgers are fighters by any standards
and many dogs will put their tails down after a beating from
Brock. These badgers were dug and tipped into coal trucks that
lay idle on the sidings on the floor of the valley, and dogs were
matched against Brock in these trucks. Tom's tales of the depression were a wonder to all. His favourite tale was of a particularly
savage badger that had been dug out in the village of Tondu and
had whipped every working terrier and fighting bull terrier from
The Ogmore to the Llynfi. Nothing would stand against this
battle scarred old boar. It made a bee line for every dog placed

on the floor of the truck, and also attacked the legs of any man slow enough not to be able to get to the top of the sides of the truck. The poor beast must have been driven insane by this senseless baiting and irritation. ' Hard times beget cruel men '. At this time Tom had a friend called Ned Evans who bred a very hard strain of Bedlington in our neighbouring valley. Ned brought a four and a half month old Bedlington puppy to watch the carnage done by Brock, and maybe pick up a trick or two. While Ned sat on the edge of the truck watching Brock pulverising another hapless victim, his terrier became excited and lunged forward toppling Ned into the truck. Brock immediately rushed Ned and he would have been quite badly bitten had not the puppy attacked the Brock with such fury that it left four of its milk teeth embedded in the badger's hide.

It is likely that much of this old fiery blood went to the wall when the show men created a finer, more elegant Bedlington. Whippets were crossed with these terriers in order ot produce a distinct roach back in the show Bedlington; much of the gameness has still been retained however—a glance at the show ring at a National show will convince any doubting Thomas of the fact. Some people still hunt the show Bedlington with considerable success. Roland Jones of Pontycymmer, Glamorgan, states that few working terriers have the courage of a Bedlington; Michael Andrews of Cumberland has terriers that are so hard that his will kill a hedgehog by biting through the spines. They are too large for most fox earths, but many hunters state they are ideally suited for badger hunting. Many people, myself included, believe that the Bedlington is far too large for most working terriers' tasks. Secondly, most Bedlingtons are notoriously mute underground, prefering to lay hold and kill the fox rather than bolt it. Most working terriers must give tongue to tell the hunter where the quarry is, but Bedlingtons tend to kill the prey rather than bolt it. This notoriously hard nature is often the death of the dog, for many will die rather than give ground to a badger. I have seen Bedlingtons take some frightful maulings from badgers.

As a breed to hybridise with greyhounds and produce all purpose lurchers, the Bedlington has many advantages. Drabble states the Bedlington is most suitable to cross with whippets to produce rabbiting lurchers, but this is not the general opinion. Greyhound/Bedlington first crosses sell very well indeed, and this alone gives some indication of their worth. I know one gypsy who travelled 300 miles to purchase a Bedlington/Greyhound puppy. The reason for the popularity of lurchers bred this way is easy to understand. Firstly, many of the hybrids are smaller and more agile than the greyhound dam—for the use of a Bedlington sire weighing 20lbs. and measuring 16″ usually ensures a reduction in the size of the lurcher. Secondly, many of the offspring inherit the soft woolly coat of the Bedlington which is excellent protection against thorns, wire and the elements. David Lloyd of Birmingham has a first cross Bedlington greyhound: the bitch has a coat so structured that one shake is enough to clear it of all surplus water and leave the dog relatively dry. Lastly, the Bedlington is a terrier—one of the gamest animals on God's earth. Some of this gameness comes through in the progeny. This makes the Bedlington lurcher a dog that tries even though the " chips are down "—an essential quality in a lurcher.

On the debit side however, some of the ugliest lurchers I have ever seen were Bedlington/Greyhound hybrids. Often the coat on the first cross looks extremely scruffy. If, however, handsome is as handsome does, this should not worry the reader. Next, many agree with Tom Jones of Lichfield who will not contemplate the Bedlington cross as terriers are notoriously hard mouthed. Dogs that are expected to thrash a fox to death are unlikely to be soft mouthed when catching a rabbit. This is not always the case, however. Ray Jones who lamps a great deal of land in Breconshire breeds and uses only Bedlington/Greyhound hybrids. Ray finds that few of the rabbits retrieved by his lurchers are damaged. Ray's dogs are scruffy to the point of being ugly but are remarkably versatile and intelligent, proof, perhaps, of the statement that the Bedlington is a multipurpose dog. Many people agree with Tom about the statement that Bedlington lurchers can be extremely hard to break to cats. Bedlingtons themselves are sadly, renowned cat killers. Tom Evans of Blaengarw, that mine of dog information, used to say that Bedlington terriers had to be brought up with cats from puppyhood to make them absolutely steady. Cats appearing on the beam are very susceptible to attack by most lurchers and Bedlington crosses find them quite irresistible.

Ray breeds his own Bedlington greyhound hybrids. Such is the fame of his stock that when he decides to sell his surplus he never has to advertise and most of his clients seem to be gypsies or tinkers. In order to produce these lurchers Ray first obtains a greyhound bitch from a local track. He usually tries to get a bitch that has been barred for fighting although any greyhound will usually do; he fights shy of dogs rejected through foot weakness. Ray says that he has seen much foot weakness inherited by puppies, and considering that he hunts some extremely rough and rocky terrain he prefers not to chance breeding-in the defect. The sire he uses comes from the S. Welsh valleys. This strain is still hunted and is very game. No written pedigree accompanies this family of Bedlingtons though most of them are probably pure Bedlington. The strain are natural workers and very quarrelsome —a quality that comes through in most of his lurchers who are quite willing to mix it with any dog that upsets them. Ray will not use a show Bedlington at any cost, as he believes that many generations of shows produces a dog with a somewhat dull edge. Neither will he use a dog which is not absolutely dead game, and he will check on the owner's stories of fox killing and badger drawing. This family of Bedlingtons are certainly no beauties but judging from the lurchers Ray produces they certainly produce the goods. Ray will never use a Bedlington bitch to a greyhound dog. "The puppies are usually too large", says Ray "and are likely to be difficult for a narrow hipped breed like a Bedlington to pass". Furthermore greyhound bitches can be begged from a track whereas a pure bred Bedlington bitch is usually quite expensive. Neither does Ray believe in excessive maternal inheritance of intelligence and guts. (Some people believe that the puppies acquire their brains and courage from the bitch—a totally fallacious idea originating among breeders of gamecocks.) "A greyhound x Bedlington is half Bedlington no matter how you mix them", says Ray, "but I would never use a show Bedlington; that would defeat the purpose. Neither would I mate a Bedlington lurcher to another lurcher", states Ray, "It has to be a first cross or nothing. I've seen damned nigh pure Bedlingtons and some pretty horrible results come from mating two Bedlington lurchers together. Get a greyhound bitch, mate her to a Bedlington dog and keep the brightest from the litter", is his advice.

Ray certainly has some outstanding dogs and they are renowned for stamina and guts. Ray tells a tale of one bitch called Blaze that took some beating. One cold December night Ray took 53 rabbits with the bitch running her on the lamp. He returned home and went to bed. Meanwhile his brother borrowed the bitch to draw some foxes being dug out by the local terrier lads. She coursed and killed three foxes that day. Meanwhile Ray who was unaware of his brother's purloining the bitch charged up his lamp battery and hunted the bitch to rabbit again that night. The old bitch was tiring a bit after I had taken 30 rabbits" said Ray, and I could not understand why. I thought she'd had a day to recover from the hunting!".

Blaze was an exceptional rabbitting dog but except by lamping she was not big enough to take hare, though she would break her heart trying to get up on one. Ray was never a hare hunting man and states that if he had wanted a hare dog he would have mated his greyhound to a deerhound. Ray deliberately bred lamping dogs though they had other uses.

One day some friends invited me to come down to Carmarthen and clear some badgers that they intended to take alive to a man in Kesteven. I wrote and told Ray I was coming down and he asked if he could come. When I arrived at his home he asked if he could bring Blaze. I was, I admit, very unhappy about this. During a badger dig the terriers are tied up and wait their turn to be entered to Brock. A lurcher walking free among them would bring paroxysms of fury from them and start some really deadly fights. Reluctantly I agreed as I hated offending an old friend. He brought Blaze who slept curled round his feet in the car. The dig was a hard one and we were all exhausted by the time the small ursine head of Brock appeared. I cursed, for he was in no position in which I could draw him. "Hang on a minute", said Ray and let slip Blaze who crawled into the earth with the stealth of a cat. She was 20 inches tall and weighed maybe 40lbs. at the most. She made many darting lunges at Brock who struck back like a snake. At last Ray shouted, "She's got him", Blaze pulled the badger out of the hole like a cork out of a bottle. She received two sharp nips under her neck for her troubles but she was otherwise unhurt. Drawing a badger which has anchored his front feet in the soil is a tremendous effort even for a man.

Blaze took fox very readily, but being only a matter of 6 inches bigger than the fox she frequently made a meal of it. One day I was hunting a copse near Pencoed with my terriers. Ray's Blaze had attacked one and so Ray kept her on a slip. My team began barking and a large dog fox slunk out unhurriedly, as if he knew my terriers were not fast enough to take him. Blaze was and Ray slipped her. A few yards from the hedge the fox realised he was not going to get away. Blaze bowled straight into the waiting fangs and gripped the fox across the loins. She shook the body frantically, but when we arrived at the scene we found her body covered with blood. At first I though she had severed the fox's jugular vein, but on examination of the tail-wagging Blaze I found that as she had grabbed the fox across the loins it had gripped the nearest thing to it, which happened to be Blaze's ear. In the rictus of death the fox still held the mangled ear between its teeth. Ear bites bleed dreadfully and a severed ear spills enough gore to saturate a dog. In the past many wolf hunters cropped their dogs ears to the skull cauterising the end of the ear to prevent bleeding. This prevented great blood loss through an ear bite during a hunt. In spite of the pain she experienced during fox hunts I never knew Blaze bark. A terrier club had been formed in Brecon and lasted only two years as the members were as quarrelsome as their dogs. Ray avoided them as he is a small active, but fragile looking man who is a little out of place in a brawl, but eventually they asked him to course foxes they had bolted and he agreed. Blaze killed over 200 by the time riot and fighting caused the club to be disbanded. Blaze was a mass of scars through Ray's contact with the Brecon club and a few of them were wounds put in by terriers who had been slipped by owners as Blaze was killing the fox. Ray is a solitary man and he breathed a sigh of relief when the club came to an end.

Few Bedlington lurchers are of use for hare. They are usually small and subsequently not big enough to get up on a hare. As a rabbitting dog and a fox killer or a general purpose dog with a lot of courage, the cross has much to commend it.

CHAPTER 14

The Bull-Terrier Lurcher

During the last few years the bull terrier lurcher has become increasingly popular. Barely a week goes by without an advertisement for bull terrier hybrids appearing in "Exchange and Mart". Along Welsh borders, and in North Wales, the bull terier greyhound is the most popular cross for producing all round lurchers. Tom, our local lurcher sage, says that along the Welsh Borders there is a saying that there are no good rough coated lurchers. While this is clearly an exaggeration it does indicate the popularity of the bull terrier cross, and such popularity can only have been brought about by the fact that the cross is extremely useful. Funnily enough few bull terrier lurchers win at the more noted lurcher shows. This however should not deter the reader. Handsome is as handsome does in the lurcher fraternity and shows are rarely if ever a true indication of the value of a lurcher.

No dog has a more varied and bloodstained history than the bull terrier. To begin at the beginning, in the year 1209 William Earl Warren watched two bulls battle it out for an in season cow. The crash of skulls and horns and the roar of the antagonists was made all the more carcophanous by the rowdly crowd who urged a pack of cur dogs on to the battling bulls. So impressed was William Earl Warren, who by modern standards would have been regarded as a bit of a sadist, that he decreed that six weeks before Christmas a maddened bull should be provided for the dogs to bait to death. The sport (if one can call bulls being ripped assunder by dogs and the contest only stopping when the bull collapsed in its own gore and entrails, a sport) caught on and a new breed began to evolve to participate in the riot. The raw material for such a breed was readily obtainable. Ban dogs, a butcher dog used for driving recalcitrant beasts to slaughter were common. These mongrel mastiffs were fiercely aggressive to both man and beast alike, and these became the ancestors of the English Bulldog.

Gradually a new breed came into existence: fierce, valiant unto death, with the nostrils set back on the muzzle so that it could breath while it held its deathlike grip. And what a grip it was. A midland butcher once owned a noted bulldog bitch who was famed for her awesome grip. One day while the dog gripped the muzzle of the roaring rearing bull, the butcher boasted he could sever the legs of the dog without the bulldog releasing its grip. Some villain heard the boast and challenged the butcher who immediately took a saw and cut off four of the dogs legs. The torso still held its deadly grip. So impressed was the mob that the butcher sold the puppies from his legless bitch for five pounds a piece. It is saddening that such a noble and valiant dog should have been owned by such a monstrous and inhuman owner.

Many owners valued their dogs highly however. During bull baits, the dogs often held the bull by the lips and nose and the rearing and tossing of the bull frequently threw the dog (who often still held the severed lips of the bull in its jaws) into the air. Idlers and wastrels from the crowd were paid to crouch beneath the falling bull dog and break the fall by allowing the dog to crash down on their backs.

Bulls were not the only animals to be baited by our inhuman ancestors. Half-tamed brown bears were brought from the continent and used for bulldogs to bait. Bears are formidable opponents and would make mincemeat of any dog, so the bears were blinded by plunging hot irons into their eyes to even the unequal contest. Then chained by the neck in the pitch blackness of their blindness, they fought off the savage attacks of the bulldogs. Such contests often resulted in dismembered dogs, but bears were rarely baited to death. They were expensive imports and properly managed could be used for up to three hundred baits before sepsis and shock carried them off.

Brutal as this appears it pales to insignificance alongside the spectacle the Midlands once offered. A contest to the death between a human dwarf called Brummy, and a ferocious bulldog Physic, was staged in the mid-nineteenth century. The contest ended with the dwarf strangling and clubbing the dog to death, after the bulldog had chewed off half the dwarf's face. Rumour has it the dwarf had qualified for such a contest by eating a live cat.

By 1835 bull baiting had become illegal, not because of the savage cruelty involved but because the new towns emerging through the Industrial Revolution were loathe to tolerate the rowdy mobs of pimps, cuts purses and thugs the baits attracted, mobs so rowdy that once when a bull could not be provided for a bait, the mob began to destroy the town. The town officials were so terrified by the mob that they provided an old horse to be torn apart by the bulldogs. Such macabre and ghastly spectacles attracted the nastiest elements of society, and 1835 saw the end of bull baiting. It was not before time. The sport had existed for six hundred bloody years and resulted in the horrendous deaths of countless animals.

Although bull baiting had become illegal the British sporting public were loathe to waste such sporting blood. Rat pits involving the slaughter of hundreds of rats by dogs in timed competitions became the rage, and the bulldogs ameliorated with the blood of faster terriers were ideal for such a sport. Billy, one bulldog terrier hybrid, once killed one thousand rats in fifty-four minutes in such a contest, but a far more sinister sport was on the horizon.

Dog fighting had always been popular in Britain and the bulldog, savage, relentless and with an awe inspiring grip, was ideal for the job. It was however, just a little slow for the task. This was easily rectified however by adding just a dash of terrier blood. The resulting hybrid became "the" fighting dog. Few pits used anything other than the bull and terrier cross for dog fighting, though a heavy Scottish type of bulldog called the Blue Paul was popular for a brief spell. Dog fighting had rules as strict as the Queensbury Rules of boxing. Dogs of equal weights were matched and the contests invariably to the death. Before a contest began the dogs were covered in milk and some official, who must have been just a trifle odd, required to lick the milk from both dogs. The operation was not as pointless as one might imagine. Many dog fighters covered the throats and stifles (where a bite could have deadly effects) with acetic acid or caustic soda which had a taste so bitter that few dogs felt happy with such chemicals in their mouths. The taster detected such malpractices. The new fighting dog which later became the Staffordshire bull terrier was a useful, though ugly animal. Many had the squashed faces of their bulldog ancestors and quite a few had dreadfully undershot mouths. Several breeders set out to improve the appearance of the breed, for dog shows were becoming popular. One such breeder, James Hinks of Birmingham, produced a more attractive animal by crossing the bull terrier with dalmatians, greyhounds and other dogs to produce the English Bull Terrier. Once while on his way to a show with his bull terrier bitch Puss, a dog fighting man chided him, saying that he had ruined the fighting qualities of the bull terrier. Hinks immediately challenged the man to a contest, Puss promptly slew her opponent and went on to win at the show.

It is of interest that Lord Orford also realised the sporting qualities of the bulldog and crossed it with his coursing greyhounds to give them fire and guts to go on when conditions became tough. Orfords famous Waterloo Cup winner Czarina was one sixteenth part bulldog.

It is not surprising that present-day lurcher breeders, seek to produce all round lurchers by crossing a dog with such fiery ancestry (the bull terrier) with the greyhound. The offspring bound to have tremendous spiritual endurance and great strength. The breeding of such lurchers is not without problems however. The greatest problem that will beset the would-be lurcher breeder who decides to breed bull terrier/greyhound hybrids is the factor which Tom, my lurcher breeding friend, describes as "wastage". Many of the litter will be far too heavy to make first class coursing or lamping dogs, and being as few people are willing to take on such dogs, most of the heavy puppies are usually put down. When the correct type 'appears in the litter however, they make exceptional coursing and lamping dogs. Tom often talks of a dog called Sonny that came from the Isle of Man. Sonny was a result of crossing a Staffordshire Bull Terrier Male (few breeders use English Bull Terriers) with a track greyhound bitch. Sonny was famous as a lamper and all-round courser. On the lamp he rarely missed a rabbit and he took some record hauls for his owner.

Even some of the heavier dogs are not without their uses. Tom Larcombe of the West Country tells an interesting story of his stud dog Tod. Tod was the result of a mating from a huge black Staffordshire Bull Terrier dog who was a noted fighter in Devonshire. He was as gentle as a lamb with people, but became a raging demon when he saw another dog. Once he had been taken to a vets to have a huge rip in his side stitched, but had attacked an alsatian in the waiting room and refused to release his grip. Eventually the vet, in fear of the life of the alsatian had been forced to chloroform the bull terrier and even then the teeth had to be prised open with an iron bar. This dog, who was clearly a throwback to the days of the old fighting dog, was mated to a track greyhound bitch. She produced eight puppies, only one of which was really suitable for use as a coursing dog. Tod was not the one. Tom was frankly disappointed by Tod's massive shape. From the photographs he resembled a rather snipey half starved mastiff. He took a few rabbits by the lamp but fewer still by day. Hares were out of the question for the dog was just not fast enough, though no one could have accused him of not trying. If only effort could have been rewarded he would have been a world beater. One night however he missed his rabbit and crashed into a barbed wire fence snapping the strand with his broad muscular chest. In the beam, the saucer-like luminous eyes of a fox appeared, and Tod collided with the fox almost by accident. Larcombe says that the fox must have put in five or six bites before Tod connected, but when he struck the fox had little or no chance. A few seconds later Tod was shaking a fox carcase that had few unbroken bones in its body. From that time on Tod wed to foxes. If one bolted he moved heaven and earth to get to it. He smashed through barbed wire, split hedges in an effort to get to his prey. Funnily enough he began to give up on "difficult" rabbits and refused to chase hares. At that time there was little or no market for skins or Tom could have made a living, pelt hunting. When Tom dug down to a fox, Tod would drag the fox out by the face though the result of such jaw to jaw encounters frequently resulted in Tod taking several bad bites from the fox. Still he was undeterred by this. With badger he was equally formidable and was used as a catch dog by local terrier men. When a badger bolted and "got through" the dog Tod would run in and throw Brock in the air. He would continue to throw the badger about until help arrived. Tom says that Tod had drawn over sixty badgers during his life and only once did he sustain a bad bite. Tod had pinned his badger and was forcing for a hold when a border terrier slipped its lead and ran in. Tod turned slightly to warn off the barking terrier and received a terrific jaw bite from Brock. The teeth of the badger actually went deep into the jaw bone and laid the throat bare. So savage was the bite that it exposed some of the windpipe. Tom says that he heard the dog whimper, saw him draw the badger in a most awkward manner and only realised the damage done some twenty minutes later when the chest of his dog became a red cascade of blood. I have heard many men boast of badger killing lurchers. If Tod failed, few dogs would have been able to kill an adult badger. Tods jaws healed well but crookedly, but it did not prevent his hunting. He ran fox for another season before he encountered roebuck. He found little difficulty in holding these delicate deer, but he was scarcely nimble enough to catch one. One of Tom's friends had a track whippet dog who would hold them just long enough for Tod to come in and get a hold. Tom later mated his lurcher to several greyhound bitches and bred some first rate all-round lurchers. Not only did they make excellent lamping and fox dogs, but some excellent hare coursing dogs resulted from these matings. One which he sold to a man in Bath is a handsome black brindle dog called Nash (after Beau Nash, the dandy of Bath). Nash is a famous hare dog in that district and is able to clear seven feet fences with almost contemptuous ease. One day while Nash was coursing a hare

around a field near a wartime aerodrome, his owner realised he
had an audience. Some tinkers were watching Nash's skill and
were obviously impressed. One approached the dogs owner and
offered to trade a lorry for the dog. The offer was refused, and
inspite of the fact that Nash was kennelled over twenty miles from
the aerodrome, that night he was stolen. Larcombe helped as
best he could to find the dog but to no avail. Seven weeks later,
however, a very footsore and tired Nash arrived on his doorstep.
The dog was half starved, but within a matter of a week or so,
was coursing hares as well as ever. Nash was as close to Tom's
dreams of the ideal lurcher as is possible. Very few creatures
could better his speed. He found even roe deer easy meat and
killed several dozen that were sold to a west country game shop.
His greatest feat however occurred on one of the west country
moors. His owner had sent him after a hare that was a little
too far distant to be fair to the dog. Still Nash had tried. He was
lost for over twenty minutes before his owner went to look for
him, only to find him latched on to a fully grown red deer stag.
The fight had gone on for a fair while and the dog was holding on
like grim death to the stag, who was on his knees with exhaustion.
Undoubtedly the grip was a result of his bull terrier ancestry.

Walt Matthew's, who hunts Mid-Wales, is almost fanatical
about his enthusiasm for the bull terrier lurcher. Walt is a
scientific lurcher breeder who considers that the first cross between
the greyhound and the bull terrier produces far too much litter
wastage. Walt's stud dog was an elderly animal who was once a
useful lamp dog. His sire was a show bull terrier sired by the
famous champion Black Monarch while his dam was a track
whippet bitch who became too big for the track and was offered
in "Exchange and Mart" as "free to a good home". Walt
found that she damaged her feet too easily for a good coursing dog
and mated her to the bull terrier. He admits most of the offspring
were "aweful" being far too heavy for what he wanted. One or
two made moderate lamp dogs but the one he kept which he
called Paddy was a different kettle of fish. Paddy was a useful
rabbitting dog working very well with ferrets. He would plunge
into the thicket bush to catch an escaping rabbit and feared
nothing. I once lost £40 to Walt in a rat catching contest in which
Paddy easily "dusted" my young terrier (I must add for my own
pride that I won the money back the next year and a bit more
besides). Paddy was a demon ratter, he would kill at a bite and
never bothered to shake. If the rat still squealed, he left it if he
knew he had put in the fatal back breaking bite. Although he was
a brilliant lamp dog, he was far too hard mouthed to be much of
a provider of saleable rabbits. Almost every rabbit he caught

was quite badly damaged. So hard mouthed was the dog, that I have seen him bite toads and kill hedgehogs. Walt never broke him to cat, inspite of savage beatings he gave the dog every time it killed one. His visits to my cottage were always a little hair raising as I own several Siamese who have the run of the place. Paddy was forced to sleep in the car. One day one of my cats jumped on the bonnet of the car, and Paddy knocked himself out by jumping against the windscreen!

Walt bred his strain of lurcher by mating Paddy to track greyhound bitches. The offspring are certainly excellent all-round lurchers. Most are fast enough for hare and the whippet blood makes them small enough and nimble enough to be excellent lamp dogs. Walt kept back several of these lurchers and swears that all are soft mouthed unlike their fearsome father. Most are however as game as the sire and will face almost anything. One of these dogs was sold to a hunter in Birmingham and used to hunt fox which abound on the tips and waste land of central Birmingham. This dog is a twenty-two inch brindle and as good looking a small lurcher as one could hope to see. The dog is very soft mouthed and will retrieve a rabbit or hare alive. Its method of tackling fox is strange. It repeatedly bowls the fox but will not put in a killing bite, though it will hold any fox that tries to escape. At the present time when fox pelts are fetching £15 a piece such a dog must be very useful for the fox pelts must be unmarked to be of value. A twenty-two inch dog seems a shade small for the ideal fox killing lurcher, but the dog has taken seventy odd foxes and is virtually unmarked. Some lurchers develop the knack of killing foxes, without receiving a bad mauling themselves. I should imagine that the coursing life of this dog is going to be short as he is run on tips where broken glass and jagged pieces of iron are found on the surface.

There are few advocates of the English Bull Terrier x greyhound hybrid. For some reason it never became a popular cross. Perhaps the English Bull's white colouration makes it unpopular with the poaching fraternity who avoid white dogs like the plague, for white dogs stick out like sore thumbs on poaching expeditions. Perhaps the fact that early English Bull Terriers were frequently deaf has something to do with their lack of popularity among the lurchermen. Whatever the reason the Staffordshire Bull Terrier is the most commonly used bull terrier to produce lurchers. There are some people who swear by the English Bull Terrier lurcher, however. Some years ago I sold quite a few Jack Russell Terriers to a coursing man in Ireland. James Creahan or Paddy Creahan as he is known, is one of the most remarkable characters I have ever met. For a long time I never met him, as I sent his dogs across to him. All I knew about him was that his hand writing was the rare old copper plate style. I imagined him a quaint old erudite schoolmaster. When he did arrive it was something of a shock. He was soft spoken, well educated—but huge! He stands six feet seven and must weigh eighteen stone. Never judge a man by his letters! Paddy breeds his own lurchers. He has tried just about every cross from collie/greyhound down to a hybrid between the bent legged Glen of Imaal terrier and a greyhound. Nothing suited him until he obtained a damaged racing greyhound bitch puppy and mated her to a fiery white bull terrier from the Ormandy strain. From these he bred his ideal dogs. Paddy believes that there is less "wastage" in the litter from an English bull terrier than from a Staffordshire bull terrier. Furthermore he he is convinced that the addition of dalmatian blood, etc., in the white Englis bull terriers make-up, makes it a brighter, more biddable dog. During my visit to Ireland to watch the Glen of Imaal show I visited Paddy in his tiny smallholding and saw his lurchers. They would appear a little heavy for top class hare dogs, but Paddy assures me that they do take hare—though it is a very long course and largely a war of attrition as they ran the hare almost to a standstill. Paddy does not "lamp" and he considers it an unsporting practice, but several of his puppies have gone to lamping men. Paddy has many letters from these men praising his dogs and what is more never needs to advertise when he has a litter. Many of his clients are tinkers who travel a few hundred miles to get a puppy. Paddy's own dogs take both fox and badger without much trouble and learn to handle Brock, keeping out of the way of his deadly "cutlery". Two of his dogs bought by a pair of Durham lads have proved brilliant all-round lurchers. Run as a pair they are useful hare dogs (though I doubt if they are good single handed hare killers) and both are remarkably good soft mouthed retrievers. In spite of their apparent docility they are demon fox dogs and have a creditable total of roe deer kills. In spite of the fact that both kennel and work together, they will not tolerate another dog near them and killed a pair of useful Lakeland terriers that upset them. Paddy tells a story about a pair of his dogs that is both interesting and tragic. He owned a very game little Glen of Imaal terrier dog, a real varmint who looks a little like a bent legged wheaten cairn terrier. These dogs are useful siezing dogs at the end of a badger dig, but being as they are invariably mute they make doubtful working terriers. Most are very quarrelsome and here begins the tale. Paddy had gone to a farm in Antrim to dig out badgers that had rolled about half an acre of corn completely flat. He had taken his Glen of Imaal terrier to "fix" or hold the badger at the end of the dig, and as a second thought had brought along the pair of bull terrier greyhounds, both fourteen months old. He had no intention of using them and just took them for the ride. It had been a very long hard dig and the terrier had fixed and held a huge sandy coloured boar badger who had fought so well that he had made mincemeat of the Russell type terriers who had gone to ground at him. The Glen of Imaal had held him at the mouth of the earth and then only after a titanic battle. Paddy had killed the boar with a spade and because the skin was quite unique he had taken the carcasse to the van with a view to skinning it when he got home. The terrier jumped in the van and was very protective about the badger, warning the two lurchers as they sniffed the body. It was Sunday lunch time and few badger diggers can resist a drink after a hard dig. It was a drink Paddy bitterly regretted. He had a warning that things were wrong when a fellow drinker had said " Your dogs are kicking up a hell of a din in that van ", but had ignored it. When he returned to the van he found his terrier and one lurcher dead and the other lurcher dying. The terrier had been too protective over the badger and his bites and warnings had upset the lurchers, who after all were fifty per cent bull terrier, not exactly the breed to take an insult lightly.

CHAPTER 15

The Whippet Lurcher

Whippet lurchers can be divided into two categories.

(a) Whippet lurchers created by crossing whippets with breeds other than sight hounds to produce a small lurcher suitable for rabbitting and lampwork.

(b) Whippet lurchers created by crossing whippets with other sight hound to reduce the size of progeny and to give increased agility and turning ability.

Firstly a little about the whippet however. There are two theories about its creation. Many believe that it was simply a bred down greyhound—a result of hybridising greyhounds with slender smooth coated terriers such as the Manchester terrier. Others believe it to be a bred up Italian greyhound, again by crossing with breeds of terrier such as the Bedlington and Manchester terrier I am inclined to believe the " bred down " greyhound theory, as the Italian greyhound was far too fragile a starting point for a working man's dog required to endure the hardship and malnutrition that hampered the working class during the times when whippet breeding started. The whippet was essentially a working man's dog. Poor men's greyhounds the early writers called them. Early whippets were probably quite simply small smooth coated greyhound lurchers. Evidence is to suggest that the first whippets were not bred for racing, but were quite simply rabbit providers for the Northern working man. Many had sufficient terrier blood to make them excellent and lightning quick rat dogs. Tom Evans of Blaengarw, whose tales of sporting dogs during the early part of this century would themselves constitute a whole book, once told me a tale concerning the rat killing ability of these early whippets. Maesteg a valley near Tom's home had some exceptionally good ratting terriers. Most were heavyjawed Sealyham types of the type favoured by the creator John Tucker

Edwards. They were light bodies, strong jawed and impervious to pain. They achieved a place in the hall of fame of all S. Welsh working terriers. During the years of the first world war a Lancashire man came to live near this district and brought with him some frail and rather fragile looking whippets. One of them ran rings round the local terriers as a rat killing dog. Tom mentions that the whippet was extremely sensitive to the cold and the wet however, but states that he had never seen a rat killing dog which performed such lightning quick rat killing exploits. The Manchester terrier, which, I believe, played a large part in the creation of the whippet was once a formidable rat pit dog, bred exclusively for the task of rat killing.

Sooner or later it is inevitable that any animal which has a turn of speed, be it pigeon, horse or dog, will be exploited as a competition animal. The whippet, once a hunting companion, now became used for racing. Traditionally the dogs were run at a rag and were thrown by the " slip " man towards the flapping rag. A more slender, faster, but more fragile dog was required for these sharp short dashes which were never the size of the course greyhounds were required to run. Specialists in this form of racing emerged in most heavily industrialised areas of the country. Staffordshire had numerous experts in conditioning these tiny dogs. Even in times of financial depression most whippet racers fed their dogs only on the best of food. It was good economic sense for dogs in first class condition could easily double the houses weekly income. Even during the bad days of the 1920's people bet considerable sums on these slender running dogs.

One of Tom's favourite tales about whippet racing concerns a great uncle of mine. He was a great character, who owned fighting cocks and dogs, which were so battle scarred, that it was concluded that he fought them. Somehow or other he acquired two houses—tiny terraced mining houses near the subsidence torn head of the valley. He was a great gambler and would bet even on two rain drops running down a window pane. He was so certain of the outcome of one whippet race that he bet one of the houses on a pale blue and white dog belonging to an eccentric mining friend of his. The day before the race he was horrified to see the dog scrounging food from the ash buckets that lined the pavements. He raced back and tried to cancel the bet but couldn't. Needless to say he lost his house and it finished him for gambling. My mother held up this curious old man as an object lesson to prevent me straying from the straight and narrow. I found Billy to be one of the most exciting and interesting old men in the village. The rest of our family faded into an anaemic

paleness besides the fascinating old renegade. Eventually my
mother stopped me visiting his house. When he lay in bed dying
of the fatal combination of silicosis and senility he asked the
doctor his chance on " making it ". His doctor answered truth-
fully, about ten to one. Even with such good odds Billy died.

In the years between the wars the whippet became popular as a
show dog. The whippet, as every sporting breed, was ruined as a
running animal by the show craze. In time he began to look more of
the part as a running dog, but the essential quality of a running dog
"heart" was lost. The old rake thin scruffy little running dog of old
was lost for ever. Furthermore during the thirties and forties the
interest in whippet racing diminished and its popularity as a show
dog increased. Soon it became very difficult to obtain dogs of the
right sort with heart and feet suitable for running those short
sharp dashes. A story will illustrate my point. Henry Rodger, a
close friend during the hectic and bizarre days I lived in the middle
of Rotherham, hunted with my terrier pack along the stretch of
rough building rubble strewn tips near Holmes. We lost many
of the rabbits we put up in fact, although the sport was exciting
I doubt if we caught more than 2% of the rabbits the terriers
chased. One day, Henry, who was sickened with the near misses,
turned up with a yearling whippet bitch. The bitch was superbly
bred and a champion studded pedigree—show champion that is.
We hunted her for about twelve months. On areas as flat as a
bowling green she would course well, but on land which was rough
or filled with rabbit hiding patches she was very indifferent.

One day a terrier man from Barnsley brought two whippet
males to hunt our rough land. They were dynamite. Both would
dash across the wasteland at a breakneck speed after an escaping
rabbit and they would hurl themselves into the most formidable
briar patches and drag out their prey. The whole performance
put Henry's neat glamorous bitch to shame. Henry watched the
whole performance impassively and bought a racing bitch a few
days later. Perhaps if we had had good coursing conditions and
flat green fields things might have been different. As it was, we
hunted a tip with jagged surfaces and pools of freshly tipped
chemicals which ate away the soles of my shoes when I stepped
in them. For these conditions a dog had to be as game as a
bantam cock. Henry's show bred whippet wasn't.

After the 1939-1945 war, interest in whippet racing began to
revive. The enthusiasm for the sport was there, but the dogs
were not. The old racing blood was nearly extinct. There was
the show blood a plenty however and for a number of years people

raced these pure bred show whippets. Some were successful, but the times were poor and few of the dogs showed any of the mad impetuosity the old racing blood showed when a rag was flapped. The show blood had to be resuscitated and there were breeders who had a good idea of how to do this.

There were two methods of creating a suitable running dog. One method was to cross the existing small number of running whippets with small greyhounds and breed from the smaller off-spring. The traditional whippet shape was lost through this hybridisation, and many racing whippet fans objected to this new type of dog competing. Many clubs passed rules that only pedigree whippets should race. Pedigrees however are easily brought from people who are concerned with the theology of making the " fast buck ". The show whippet could not compete with this new hybrid and it fell out of favour on most tracks.

Another method of creating a racing whippet was to hybridise whippets with fiery breeds of terrier. Bull terrier crosses were common in the Midlands and many 1/16 part bull terrier whippets won on the whippet racing tracks. Other breeders keen not to lose the traditional whippet shape used fiery Bedlington terriers. The first cross was obviously not eligible, as most were rough coated. They had the necessary fire however and second and third crosses (back mating to whippets) were often the ideal hybrids. Ben Bradshaw, a whippet breeder just north of the Black Country, once offered me a whippet puppy bred from five generations of pure whippets that had a silky top knot and a slightly broken coat. Such throwbacks are rare however. Ben says that the strain is probably 1/32 part Bedlington and that the first crosses from which the strain arose were used as small rabbit lurchers. Many of the studs used to create the strain were lamp-ing dogs. Another racing whippet strain bred just south of Birm-ingham is reputed to be bred from an ugly strain of running whippet with just a dash of Irish terrier. This strain sometimes throws a puppy with some coarse guard hair along the spine. Early on in the breeding of this strain the whippet racers had some considerable trouble because of the pugnacity of this strain which were as keen to fight as they were to run.

Many lurcher breeders use the whippet to cross with various other gaze or sight hounds to reduce size and to increase agility in the offspring. Greyhound/whippet hybrids are of course the most common. The offspring are smaller than greyhounds and are usually fairly agile. One criticism of this type of lurcher is that they often have bad feet—feet which get damaged by running over rough country. I know one lamping man from near Derby who swears by this cross however. Again this man breeds his own lurchers as he believes that most lurcher breeders are not exactly accurate in the way they describe their dogs breeding. He goes on to say, any small smooth coated lurcher is referred to as a whippet greyhound hybrid. Tom Jones, our local Lichfield lurcherman, is of the same opinion, Tom goes as far as to say " a fortune awaits the legitimate, truthful lurcher breeder ". My Derbyshire friend has had good results obtaining a heavy track greyhound bitch and a racing whippet dog. As he is a man who takes game by lamping, he avoids using either a greyhound or a whippet that is predominantly white. He also destroys any white puppies from the mating as they are hard to sell and dangerously conspicious by night. He does however have considerable trouble with foot ailments, but he has his dogs treated by the local greyhound track vet who is a marvel with knocked-up feet. Bruce keeps three bitches and lamps two every night, resting the third. His hauls of rabbits taken by night are impressive. One story however does seem to indicate that some of these hybrids do have defective feet, Bruce had obtained a legal lamping place in the Leicetershire mining district of Moira. Moira has many waste piles that are full of sharpened, dangerous pieces of shale. Bruce ran this area for a week and had to lay up his dogs for nearly a month as a result of the pounding the feet took. Another of Bruces theories is that the useful life span of a lurcher bred from two sight hounds hybridised together is fairly short. Most burn themselves out in about two active seasons says Bruce.

In spite of much search and effort I have been unable to find anyone who breeds lurchers by hybridising saluki's with whippets. This crossing may well provide a useful type of lurcher. The whippet might well reduce the size of the saluki and the saluki blood may give the cross the good feet and stamina which seems to be lacking in the whippet. I am surprised that this hybrid is not more popular. It seems to have all the qualities of the all round lurcher. It would be small enough to be a useful lamping dog and yet large enough for hare. The offspring would probably have a great deal of stamina from the saluki parent. However the saluki is the most intractable dog and many hunters avoid saluki blooded dogs for this reason. I put the idea of this cross to several lurchermen but few were enthusiastic about the prospect of breeding such a hybrid.

One occasionally sees Afghan and Borzoi/whippet hybrids advertised but these are most uncommon. I have occasionally seen deerhound whippet crosses advertised. This cross may be

of some use as the whippet may well reduce the cumbersome
nature of the deerhound and retain its good feet and stamina. The
mating of a deerhound dog to a whippet bitch could produce some
dangerous effects when the bitch came to whelp however.

The second type of whippet lurcher has now to be discussed
—that is the cross of whippets with dogs other than sight hounds.
The most popular breed to hybridise with whippets is of course the
collie. What is aimed at here is the speed and agility of the whippet
combined with the sagacity and stamina of the collie. Again it
must be stressed that the most suitable type of collie to use is
the hard, tough little border collie as yet unruined by show
breeders. John Lane of Northampton is renowned for the breeding of this cross. John used track whippets which are given to him
when they completed their useful working life. John crosses these
with a collie dog that was bred on the Brecon Beacons. He has
little trouble in selling the puppies from this breeding, the average
size of which is about 20″, John states that this cross make very
useful ferreting dogs and useful lampers. They are of course far
too small and heavily built for hare hunting. Three of John's
puppies have also won obedience tests which speaks highly of
their intelligence and trainability. John lamps small fields in
country where patches of gorse and bramble abound. What he
requires is a smallish fast dog with great turning ability and a
great deal of stamina. He breeds only this cross as it seems to be
the only type of lurcher that suits the country he hunts. At one
time John hunted pure or relatively pure bred track whippets. He
found that not only did these tire easily but they were not nearly
biddable enough to make first class coursing and poaching dogs.
He tried crossing these whippets with a variety of breeds including
poodles and bull terriers, but he finds that the collie makes the
most suitable breed to mate with whippets. Many of his lurchers
are so soft mouthed that they will retrieve a rabbit alive. One of
his most interesting tales concerns one night when he was lamping a rabbit infested patch of scrub near Peterborough. His dog
ran into the beam and picked up a shreaking screaming animal
that John first thought was a young rabbit. As the dog came
nearer a strange stench hit John's nose. His dog was carrying a
live unharmed hob polecat ferret who was decidedly annoyed by
his rough handling. The dog achieved this feat without being
bitten. One of John's puppies was sold in Lancashire to a noted
north country character and first class lamp man. In the fields
in this district rats abound and feed alongside the rabbits soon as
darkness falls. The dog would retrieve live rats to hand without
harming them and also without them biting him.

Another popular cross appears to be the Whippet/Bedlington terrier hybrid. This cross is bred to put fire into whippet blood and dogs from this breeding are often exceedingly game. A childhood friend of mine had a Bedlington whippet hybrid that would not only course rabbits but would go to ground on fox or badger. It was also an exceedingly good rat dog and performed some incredibly agile kills, hunting rat in the banks of the filthy brook that ran at the bottom of my mining valley home. The bitch was about sixteen inches high and could get down some very small earths. Like a number of Bedlington lurchers she was absolutely vicious with cats. Such was her skill at killing cats that people began to complain and my friend was forced to get rid of this super little hunting dog. I learnt much from his example. There are no prizes for cat killing. It will eventually cause a great deal of trouble for both man and dog.

One of the most useful whippet lurchers I ever saw was a result of a chance mating. At one time I bred an exceedingly hard and tough strain of working Jack Russell. They were rough coated, straight legged, but very ugly and notoriously mute when they met their quarry underground. Most would kill a fox fairly quickly and they were also terrific rat killers. The cottage in which I now live, was bought from bets I won with one of these dogs at rat killing contests. The strain had its faults however. They were so hard and tough that they would not give ground to a badger and they were frightfully mauled as a result of encounters with Brock. One dog I bred, I sold to a hunting man in Burntwood. He had all the failings of the strain and in addition to the usual faults he was a canine Lothario. Most of the mongrels in Burntwood looked like him. He was impossible to keep in when bitches came in season and would pine and fret if chained up or bite a hole through a solid oak door. One day he was found tied to a nesh and elderly whippet bitch belonging to a lady who lived in the same street. The bucket of water tipped over the mating pair and the visit to the vet who promptly injected the bitch with a hormone to kill all the puppies concerned, only partly worked. She whelped one male puppy nine weeks later.

This puppy was, I think, sold for a pound to a local poaching man who fancied his terrier cum whippet appearance. He grew up to be the best ferreting dog I have ever seen, although he would never have won a prize in a lurcher show as he was probably the most ugly dog I have ever encountered. He had, however the most incredible nose. When he marked an earth it was time to put a ferret down and place the nets. He was never wrong. When a ferret killed underground he would mark the spot as well as any ferret detecting device. If his owner missed netting a hole he would stand by the hole and paw it gently to attract his master's attention. I have never known a dog so " sympatico " with a hunter. Once when a ferret bolted a rabbit which hit the nets another bolted behind it to the now unnetted holes. He held the netted rabbit with his feet and neatly grabbed the bolting rabbit. When a ferret strayed off into the undergrowth he would carry the ferret back unharmed. He was never known to damage a net or hurt a ferret and in spite of his terrier blood he never bruised a rabbit. In fact he was never known to make a kill during his entire life. He let rats bolt through the nets unhindered, in fact he had a mental dread of rats and would stand out of the way to let one pass. He had been bitten as a small puppy by a big doe rat and had never forgotten the experience. His fame as a rabbiting dog was legendary and numerous lurcher and whippet bitches were mated to him. He was a one off job however, a dog made and then the mould broken. All his puppies were quite useless.

Once while netting a rabbit warren, his owner noted that one hole had been deeply excavated. Rabbits are traditional burrowers and often dig just for the sheer hell of it. His lurcher began to paw one of the holes frantically with a sort of berserk enthusiasm that was totally foreign to the dog and then, sin of sins, he began to give tongue—the arch sin for a ferreting dog for it tips off the rabbit that there is something nasty afoot above ground. The dog poked his head into a bolt hole and began to bay. It was a frantic staccato bay which did not stop even when his owner rapped him with a stick. Suddenly the nets were thrown by a young boar badger that exploded from the earth. In spite of his fear of rats and the panic of its first encounter with a Brock, the the dog ran Brock for nearly half a mile, barking and trying to get in a bite on the badgers leathery hide. Badgers move about as fast as an average man can run, but are so tank like that a terrier/whippet lurcher is most unlikely to be able to stop one. The fact that the dog returned without even a bite is a bit of a mystery.

During my time in the North Country I once bred a litter of useful whippet lurchers. My old friend Hardy once came to me in a bit of a quandary. One of my friends had raced a rather flashy little whippet bitch quite successfully for about two seasons. One day she had tried to jump a stone wall after a cat, and smashed a leg. The leg had healed quite well, and to all intents and purposes she was as good as new—except when she ' opened up ' on a track. When required to dash at nearly forty miles an hour the damage became obvious. She was as game as a bantam cock, but with one leg that packed up periodically she was as useful as a broken anvil. Hardy's friend dumped her on Hardy's doorstep and asked to get rid of her for him. In spite of Hardy's lack of concern for a fighting cocks agony, he was reluctant to put down this beautiful little bitch who was a grand-daughter of his bitch Fly. Hardy had no qualms about using my place as Battersea Dogs Home and as I had a fair amount of kennel space he asked me to take on the bitch. Much as I protested that I was a terrier breeder and I had no use for a crippled whippet, Hardy insisted I took her. She was no fighter and caused me no problems with my terriers.

About three weeks after I had her she came in season and two of my rat hunting friends asked me to mate her to a noted Staffordshire bull terrier dog that lived in Rotherham. This dog was a veritable tiger and would draw badgers in spite of the savage bites it received. It would literally pulverise a fox and was a useful rat killer. Once I had tried one of my terrier bitches in a rat killing contest against the bull terrier. She was far faster to the punch and much more adept at rat killing, but as soon as she killed a rat the bull terrier attacked her. I withdrew her from the contest as the beast would have killed her. He had the most tremendous bite I have ever encountered and literally crunched the rats he killed. I have frequently heard the crack of bones as he killed a rat. He never shook—the bite was enough. As a brawling rat killer he was ideal. As a stud dog he was hopeless. I spent nearly four long and exasperating days trying to get him to serve the bitch. When at last he managed to mate her he tied to her with a look of total bewilderment on his silly cod like face.

The bitch produced a litter of five fawn and white puppies I was strictly a terrier man at the time and I could not wait to give the puppies away to my friends. Only three went to hunters. These were like rather heavily built whippets and had little of the sires coarseness. This was a bit surprising as I imagined the offspring would be downright ugly. All three puppies were useful rat killers by the time they were seven months old and I had some fine sport, hunting a huge tip near Swinton, Yorkshire. They were as fast as greased lightning and performed some incredible acrobatic tricks, taking rats in the air.

Two of these puppies made useful ferreting dogs. One also became a useful dog, driving game to the long net. This dog once held a fully grown dog fox that tried to slip through the long net. As it was only about 17" at the shoulder the skirmish with a fox could have gone either way. When I left the district I gave the whippet bitch away and never repeated the mating. I feel that if I had kept one of these puppies and mated it to a small greyhound bitch I could have bred a very useful all-purpose lurcher. As general purpose dogs the bull terrier whippet hybrids I bred were far too slow for general coursing work, but made excellent rabbit dogs.

While in Ireland for the Misneac Teastas or certificate of dead gameness, an award given to terriers who are prepared to face heavy quarry, I saw an interesting pair of lurchers that resembled nineteen inch greyhounds. They had been bred from a large whippet bitch from racing stock, but the bitch herself had never raced. She would run hare well and had numerous kills to her credit. The bitch was glamourous enough to pass for a show whippet, but even in " running condition " she must have weighed thirty-five pounds. Somewhere in her ancestry, and not too far distant, was greyhound blood. She had been mated to a large and rangy kerry blue terrier of non-pedigree stock, but obviously pure bred. This dog had been an excellent vermin dog and had eventually been used on a badger bait—an illegal practice by any standards. He was so hard that he refused to give ground—a fatal error with Brock—and he had his lower jaw sheared off as if snipped by giant metal cutters. His owner had tried to keep him alive, but the vet had advised him to put the dog down. He lived nearly two weeks before sepsis and starvation carried him off.

His puppies were also very game—too game in fact for they would allow no other dog near them. They were also very keen on attacking children and brought numerous complaints back to their owner. In the end he had to muzzle both when he took them out for exercise. They were as deadly with cats and would hunt them as readily as they hunted rabbit. The dogs were both totally unbroken to ferret and were touchy with stock. To their credit they were excellent dogs for working cover, and were extremely keen on rabbits. Both retrieved well, but often fought over the ownership of a rabbit, I feel that they might have made useful dogs if they had been owned by someone else, but they had easily mastered their young owner.

CHAPTER 16

Sundry Crosses

A poet called Robert Browning once said " A man's reach should exceed his grasp or what's a heaven for ". In other words a man should constantly strive towards perfection. Most of the lurcher breeders sense the imperfections of their dogs and most constantly strive to get an animal that is just a bit better than the last. Some endeavour to produce their ideal beast by a series of random crosses. Others like Jimmy Keeling, go about it in a scientific way, but few lurcher men have not at some time in their lives, not tried to find some secret and often outlandish cross to produce the perfect animal. Apart from the crosses I have mentioned there are several less orthodox ways of producing lurchers.

When I was a boy a popular cross in the district around my home were retriever/greyhound crosses. There was good reason for breeding this type of lurcher. Retrieving breeds rate fairly highly in the lists of canine intelligence and the progeny of a retriever greyhound cross are usually fairly bright. Furthermore retrievers are used for fetching back shot game and as no one wants badly mangled pheasants, partridge and hares, retrieving breeds had to be soft mouthed. Furthermore retrieving breeds are usually excellent water dogs as most were evolved for retrieving game from water. The resulting lurchers were excellent all-round dogs. About thirty years ago the most popular retriever used to breed lurchers was the golden—an exceptionally soft mouthed, good nosed type of breed. In addition to the other qualities common to all retrievers it was considerably lighter in build than the labrador and therefore produced a more athletic lurcher. Few of the first crosses were fast enough for hare, however, and most breeders mated the first cross retriever/greyhound males to a greyhound bitch. The resulting progeny are often excellent. Some years ago I went with Tom Evans to Merthyr Mawr, Near Bridgend, to see a breeder who specialised in the cross. The dogs seemed very level and resembled slightly heavy broken coated greyhounds. The dogs were excellent general purpose dogs. Most would retrieve game shot by the breeder and everyone showed no fear of entering the turbulent waters of the flooded river Ogmore to retrieve a dummy. Tom was of the opinion that these were the best lurchers in Britain for general purpose hunting. I saw the breeder drop a glove without the lurcher noticing it. A mile or so further on he sent the lurcher to recover it which it did with great ease. Retrieving breeds have always interested me as they have a character and sagacity that is all their own.

The Labrador is sometimes used to create lurchers though the first cross Labrador greyhound is usually far too heavy to be much use as a coursing dog. Second generation crosses are usually a far more trim and fleet looking animal. Again the dogs are usually all very soft mouthed. This is not always the case however. Some years ago I went badger digging in Lincolnshire and had a very good sporting week. One of the group owned a black first cross labrador greyhound who was a demon. He was very touchy with my terriers and followed up the warning growl with a savage mauling if my dogs persisted in annoying. I saw this hard bitten, badly scarred old dog draw many badgers from earths and pull down several that had bolted. He was also an excellent fox dog and would bowl and kill a fully grown dog fox as well as any lurcher I have ever seen. I carry a permanent reminder of this dog. While we were digging he was chained to a nearby fence, I went back to fetch a pick that lay too near to his owner's coat. As I bent down he dealt me a savage bite across my head, a bite that nearly lifted my scalp. It required six stitches and a considerable amount of hair shaved off my head to get the wound fixed. Labradors of course often make exceptionally good guards. At one time the Metropolitan Police used labradors as police dogs. The other retrieving breeds, the curly coated and the flat coated retriever are now fairly rare, and seldom appear in the lineage of modern lurchers.

I have in my possession a letter from a man who has bred some very useful lurchers from a first cross bearded collie/greyhound. Bearded collies are the last of the herding dogs to attract the interest of the show fraternity and many still have the hardiness and brain power that made them such useful herding dogs. My neighbour breeds this attractive breed that resembles a miniature Old English sheepdog. His dogs do remarkably well at obedience tests and retrieve as well as most Spaniels. These attributes coupled with the fact that the collies have a very good protective coat, make it a useful breed to cross with a greyhound. Perhaps the only reason why such hybrids are rarely seen is that the Bearded Collie is far from common. From what I have seen they deserve to be popular.

Afghans and Borzois are sometimes crossed with greyhound to produce coursing lurchers. Neither breed can claim to be very intelligent nor very tractable so the purpose of this cross eludes me somewhat. The Afghan is merely a very heavily feathered edition of the Saluki and America boasts a few coursing champion Afghans. I have only seen one Afghan/greyhound hybrid and that however was surprisingly tractable. Nuttall of Clitheroe sometimes has a Borzoi/greyhound lurcher for sale, but I have not met anyone who has experience at coursing this elegant type of lurcher. Borzois (the name means swift, in Russian) were originally used for coursing wolves and foxes. Ghengis Khan was said to have owned dogs that resembled the modern Borzoi. Perhaps suitable fox killing lurchers could be bred from such a cross.

Irish Wolfhounds/greyhound hybrids are far from common though I have seen one or two at lurcher shows. They are usually a little too large for most lurcher men and many resemble pure bred Scottish deerhounds. The most elegant lurcher I have ever seen was a result of such a cross and its beauty was only marred by the fact it stood 32 inches at the shoulder. Such a dog would be at a great disadvantage against a 25-26 inch lurcher in the coursing field. Though it is likely the sheer size and biting power would have made the dog a useful fox hunting lurcher. There is little to gain in using a wolfhound stud when one could obtain the services of a lighter, more suitable deerhound, just as easily.

Airedale/greyhound crosses are fairly common in Glamorgan. Ray Morgan's of Severn Sisters is most enthusiastic about the cross. Most of the dogs bred near Ray's district, appear to be black broken coated dogs and have a great deal of fire. The Airedale is of course the largest of the terriers. The breed was created as a ratting terrier along the river Aire. Most authorities believe that the early Airedales were a result of crossing fighting bull terriers with otter hounds and refining the progeny by judicious mixture of Irish terrier blood. The original Airedale were very fiery. Many were used as fighting dogs and acquitted themselves well against such breeds as Staffordshire Bull Terriers. The hound blood gives the Airedale an excellent nose and few are found lacking in guts. One family, the Oorang strain, has been used on bear, wolf, mountain lion and bobcat in America. The noted big game hunter, Ben Lilly, refrained from using Airedales as they were invariably so courageous that they met with early deaths when used for hunting large predators. Ray states most of the Airedale lurchers he has seen are very classy and do the job well. They will usually tackle fox and badger well enough and make quite useful coursing dogs. Ray says that the mating of a first cross Airedale/greyhound to a good coursing greyhound, produces stuff that is hard to beat, for the further cross gives added fleetness and still preserves much of the terrier fire. Jimmy Keeling discussed such a cross when I visited his premises. He is of the opinion that an Airedale cross might be a very viable proposition. Tom Jones of Lichfield, however, says that he is decidedly unhappy about Airedale lurchers as they are by reputation usually hard mouthed. Still Airedales are extremely versatile dogs and can be used for a variety of purposes.

A cross that has always intrigued me and is one that I intend to breed is the Irish terrier greyhound cross. This cross has much to commend it. The Irish terrier was bred as a guard and vermin destroyer. Most are extremely courageous and are synonymous with blind courage. Even the most inbred show strains still have a great deal of hunting instinct and will usually tackle fox and badger without a deal of encouragement. Most are impressive guards. The Irish terrier has a rough water proof coat that is very weather resistant. A friend of mine in Whittington has a male Irish terrier that hunts well and is so hard that it will kill hedgehogs by biting through the spine. The Irish terrier is also considerably lighter and smaller than its cousin the Airedale, so is probably more suitable for breeding lurchers. Furthermore the Irish terrier is one of the few terrier breeds that is mute. This makes them useless for work underground, though the silence is a thing to be desired in a lurcher, particularly one that is used for hunting land where the hunter has no permission. Alan Liversage of the Home Counties, has such a lurcher and is well pleased with the dog, the dog is tractable, very obedient and will " split a hedge " to get to its quarry. Alan's dog is a little heavy for hare coursing, but is a first class lamping lurcher. Surprisingly the dog is soft mouthed and will return rabbits to hand undamaged. He is also " mustard " on foxes and once killed five in one night. I feel that this dog, mated to a pure greyhound bitch, might well breed the ideal lurcher, and I hope one day to breed such a hybrid myself.

Another fiery Irish terrier is the Kerry Blue. This breed is very old and is multi-purpose. Not only was the dog used for killing foxes and drawing badger, but many possessed herding instinct, enough to make them useful sheep and cattle dogs. They were also sufficiently fiery to be used as fighting dogs. I once attended a dog fight when two Kerry Blues fought to the death. The coarse long hair and thick hides make them difficult dogs to kill and the fight lasted well over an hour, when both dogs seemed near to dropping with exhaustion. Neither had made such damage on the other until one crunched his opponents stifle and proceeded to butcher the cripple at will. I detest such contests though I could not help admiring the courage of this formidable and destructive terrier. The Kerry might well be a useful starting point of the creation of a sporting lurcher. He is long coated and has a very thick hide that is almost tear proof. Furthermore it is probably one of the most versatile terriers. Many are capable of obedience test work to the highest level. Kerry's also impart a high degree of courage to any cross. During my stay in Ireland I saw a Kerry draw a forty pound badger from the mouth of an earth, and in spite of the tremendous damage inflicted by the badger the dog succeeded in its task. I examined the dog's macerated jaw after the dig and found the bone had been broken in two places. In spite of this, the Kerry had not made a single cry of pain. Few breeds can absorb such punishment as this formidable terrier. The Kerry lurcher is not uncommon in Ireland, but is relatively rare in the rest of Britain. A litter of first cross Kerry Blue/greyhounds I saw in Antrim were magnificent, they were blue black colour and resembled miniature deerhounds. I have yet to see more appealing and bright lurcher puppies. Alan Brent of Cumberland bought one of these puppies and the dog proved an admirable worker. It was really keen on rabbit and would break its heart to get up on a hare. Furthermore the combination of this blue black lurcher and Alan's working Lakeland accounted for 56 large fell foxes during the 1974-75 winter. Alan says that he has seen the dog work in very bad conditions with icicles hanging from its coat, yet after an hour's rest and food, the dog was ready to go again. One curious fault about the dog was that it was a cryptochid and was unable to breed because of this peculiarity. A pity really as it seemed to be a worthwhile line to continue. This dog has won numerous first prizes at lurcher shows. It stands twenty-five inches at the shoulder and would easily pass for a small deerhound/greyhound hybrid. Alan's only criticism of this dog is that he will not tolerate another male dog near him and is particularly spiteful to strangers who try to handle him. This is strange as he has yet to bite a judge at a show.

A cross that has attracted a deal of publicity lately is the Alsatian/greyhound lurcher. The reason for this publicity is that one lurcher owner has used such a hybrid to kill 180 Père Davids and other deer, worth a total of £12,000 and received a sentence of six months for this and other offences. This slaughter is rather a pity for the deer has been extinct in the wild for 3,000 years. As the flesh of this deer is reputed to have a curious musky taste, it is of interest where our poacher found a market for the kills. Roe deer, roughly the same size, finds a ready market, so perhaps it is just as easy to sell this rare and beautiful import. This crime although inclined to be monstrous, is perhaps proof of the versatility of this dog. I know one gamekeeper in Doncaster who will only breed this cross. Alsatians are highly intelligent dogs and, as they are used as shepherds, possess a great deal of hunting instinct. One Alsatian, owned by a school caretaker in Rotherham, made short work of several foxes which crossed the school playing fields.

John Benton, a close friend of mine, once considered the cross as he has a formidable Alsatian called Max, and Max is not wanting in hunting ability. The dog hunts rabbits well and will crash through the thickest of cover. John decided against the cross when he saw an Alsatian greyhound cross that was far too heavy for coursing.

I know of one such hybrid in the Black Forest of Germany that is an extremely useful dog. His owner must have been very lucky in his choice of puppy as the dog resembled a rather heavily built greyhound, the only hint of his Alsatian sire being in his somewhat peculiar ear carriage. This dog achieved considerable fame amongst local sportsmen and his owner was offered the equivalent of £200 for him. He would track wounded deer and was very clever at turning the extremely dangerous wild boar of the Black Forest. He was light enough to do reasonably well on hares and was a useful provider of rabbits for his owner. The dog had quite a remarkable nose and was such a ferocious guard that his owner would leave his keys in the car and offer the car to anyone who could drive it away with the dog inside. No one ever took up his offer for the dog became a raging demon when anyone touched the car door.

I tend to agree with John Benton however, for many of the progeny of such a cross are far too heavy for the average coursing man.

While in Germany I saw a number of extremely unusual poodle cross greyhound hybrids. Many of these were extremely attractive and useful dogs. The reader should forget the diminitive toy and minature poodles and consider the enormous standard poodle which was quite popular in Germany during the 1960's. The standard poodle was once a very useful breed. Not only did hunters use them to retrieve wounded game but fishermen would frequently use these wonderfully aquatic dogs to take messages from ship to shore. In spite of its comical appearance, the poodle

is rated as one of the most intelligent dogs. Circuses make use
of them because of their learning ability as much as their comical
appearance. The poodle greyhound cross is uncommon in Britain
as standard poodles are relatively rare. Still as a basis for creating a general purpose lurcher the breeder might do well to consider
the dog. Every poodle lurcher I have ever seen resembled a
poodle coated greyhound. All had hard protective coats which
rarely moulted. Most needed stripping however to prevent their
coats becoming a disastrous tangle. Such coats can be a nuisance
as the fur becomes clogged with mud, sodden with water and a
dog in this condition looks decidedly unhappy. A properly
stripped coat however is very resistant to brambles and thorns.
Most poodle lurchers are bright and adaptable, but I know of no
one who breeds this hybrid to the exclusion of all other types of
lurcher.

Another cross that became popular for about two years during
the 1960's was the English or German pointer/greyhound hybrid.
Pointers and setters are dogs with a reputation for immense
stamina. In America, where the pointer is the most popular field
trial dog, the dogs are trialed from sunrise to sunset in conditions
which vary from intense early morning frost to the blistering heat
of the noon. The breeder who intends producing this hybrid
should read the famous " Dumbell of Brookfield " to get some
idea of the stamina required by these field trial dogs. There are
however a few reasons why this cross does not make a popular
lurcher.

1. The pointer is required to point its prey. Pointing is an
adaptation of the wild instinct of hesitating before the wild dog
pounces. Foxes frequently point too before seizing a rabbit or a
bird. It is believed this pointing has a mesmerising effect on the
quarry. Whether this is so has yet to be proved, however. The
hunter should consider whether there is a trait he wishes to breed
in his lurcher. It is possibly useful for catching squatting rabbits,
but its use is a little limited.

2. The pointer is a hunter of feathered game and is con-
sequently an air scenting breed. Sometime ago foxhound blood
was introduced into the English pointer and the result was
disastrous until this ground scenting dog was bred out of the
bloodlines. Is an air scenting trait the quality a lurcher man
wishes to breed in his dogs? I would think possibly not. There
are probably a few useful pointer greyhound hybrids about, but
I should imagine that there are many not so useful hybrids in

existence. The German pointer is required to retrieve as well as point and possibly this would be a slightly more useful breed to hybridise with the greyhound.

Beagle/greyhound lurchers are becoming a great deal more popular each year. The reason for this is obvious. Not only has the beagle an excellent nose, but it has incredible stamina. Beagles are natural hunters of hares and unlike coursing dogs who kill hare after relatively short course, a beagle may hunt a hare for a whole day. Once after following the private pack of George Manners, which had hunted the hare for about four hours, I found a large eight pounds hare crouched in a hedge and bleeding from the nostrils as a result of the exertion. Breeders who contemplate breeding this cross should remember that it is much better to use the rather gaunt working beagle, rather than the more attractive and refined show beagle. Tom Jones of Lichfield speaks highly of this cross. Some excellent beagle greyhound crosses are bred in Ireland and they find a ready market in the Midlands. Tom has watched several of these dogs work, says all are tireless workers even over bad terrain such as the rocky walled district around Buxton. Should one lose sight of the hare they have enough of the scent hunting ability of the beagle to fall back on. Tom remarked that he saw this dog hunt as a team with another very fast lurcher of exclusively sight hunting crosses. Few hares escaped the combination of this superb tracking dog and this noted courses. Many of the people who breed this cross freely admit to a deal of wastage in the litters. Many are far too heavy to make useful coursing dogs and have to be destroyed or given away. A second generation mating, using one of these hybrids to a greyhound would probably remedy the problem of coarseness however.

Since the publication of the rather quaint book " Rebecca the Lurcher " sight-hound/scent-hound crosses have become quite popular. Rebecca was a cross between a foxhound male and a greyhound female and was a fairly consistent hare courser. In the last few years since the book was published, numerous foxhound/greyhound crosses have appeared in the advertisement pages of the " Exchange and Mart ". Foxhounds, at least the modern foxhound, have a reasonable amount of greyhound blood bred in them. The early hounds were heavy, ungainly and kept for their scenting ability and also for their musical voice. The dogs were too slow for the sport of fox hunting or for the type or fox hunting that has become popular today. Greyhound blood was introduced, and a faster, sleeker hound came about as a result of the cross.

Andrew Caine, who breeds Lakeland and border terriers and hunts them to fox, once bred a very useful litter of lurchers from using a fell hound male onto a coursing greyhound female. Fell hounds are lighter and faster than most of the fox hounds and are probably more suitable to use to breed lurchers. Andrew bred six puppies all of which were a uniform tan colour and resembled greyhounds with slightly pendulous ears. Andy distributed these to friends and kept a careful check on their proress. The dogs were roughly 26″ tall and the bitches all slightly smaller. So uniform were these that Andy has decided to try to produce his own strain of lurcher. All these puppies made reasonably good hare coursing dogs but lacked a little in speed. Courses became a war of attrition, for the dogs kept on running the hare long after most lurchers would have tired. His best dog coursed and hunted hare for over an hour over rough fell country. When the hare outdistanced the dog the lurcher tracked it by nose, until it found the hare again. This dog specialised in this form of hunting and often pushed a hare until it disappeared into pipes or took to the water of the nearby river. Andy is intending to mate this dog to a greyhound bitch, keep a stud dog from the mating and mate the stud to its own aunts. i.e., the sisters of its own sire. The dogs and bitches made excellent fox killers. At that time prior to 1973 Andy used his terriers for badger digging and every lurcher bred from his first mating would draw and hold badger. The whole litter lacked little in courage.

Ray Morgans of Severn Sisters, Glamorgan and a great gleaner of information about lurchers and lurcher men, has just visited my cottage. Ray states that hunting men in the Rhondda and adjacent valleys have nearly perfected a very useful strain of heavy lurcher that has come about as a result of crossing the fiery tempered Welsh hound with greyhounds and adding just a dash of Bedlington blood. A rough, tough, sturdy dog, capable of taking on heavy quarry of any sort has come about as a result of this hybridising. All have slightly pendulous ears as a result of the foxhound and Bedlington origin. All these dogs are a a little heavy for hare, but are demons at fox and badger hunting. Ray says that these lurchers seem impervious to pain. The ones I have seen are rather unsightly, but look very useful dogs. Most seem to indicate that additional greyhound blood might produce a faster more useful dog without losing any of the pluck of the existing lurchers.

Some twenty-five years ago I saw a very attractive litter of Staghound/greyhound hybrids. The Staghound is an interesting breed, I believe it was one of the earliest scent hunting hounds to enter the country. Both the Normans and the Angerin Kings were passionately fond of hunting and regarded the stag as the sable quarry. Such hounds, which resembled large coarse coated giant foxhounds, were hunted in packs to deer and probably wolf. It is unlikely the Saxon kings favoured the scent hunting breeds as much as the sight hunting breeds, and there is little indication that the breed existed in Britain before the Norman conquest. This breed was the ancestor of the foxhound and until recently large foxhounds were often drafted into staghound packs. What is interesting is the fact that though the Normans are credited with bringing the Staghound to Britain, the Mabinogion, a very ancient Welsh book that predates even the Saxon legend of Beouwolf mentions white hounds that were used for stag hunting. The hounds usually had a magical origin and were frequently the property of semi-deities or rulers of some Celtic Hell. These legends have survived and passed into modern magic for the Demonologists regard the hound as one of the creatures of Hell. A litter of Staghound/greyhound hybrids bred near Treorchy had a curious history. The sire was an excellent stag hunting dog from the West Country. In his fourth or fifth season he had run a red deer and cornered it. The stag had damned nigh dis-embowelled the dog and ripped off one ear and taken out an eye. He was no use to the stag hunting fraternity as his speed had left him. I think he must have changed hands about six times before he came to rest in the Welsh valleys. Several people used this dog and he bred a lot of useful though very tall puppies. Stag-hounds are of course very large foxhounds, not deerhounds. The name stag hound applied to deerhounds is a misnomer. As a fox hunting dog this cross probably takes some beating. Staghounds are getting scarce—at least with the outlawing of deerhunting looming on the horizon. The only problem of using a sight hound scent hound cross is that neither are particularly gifted with canine intelligence. The offspring may be somewhat brighter than the parents for in addition to hybrid vigour a peculiar kind of intelligence is acquired through this cross breeding. Hybrids between sight hounds and scent hounds start out at a decided disadvantage however. On the credit side no breeds are superior to the scent hunting breeds in stamina.

This cross has been tried frequently in America. For the past ten years I have written and supplied terriers to the Bains brothers whose father acutally knew Ben Lilly and Teddy Roosevelt. The father made a living hunting predators along the Texas frontiers. For the heavy game such as bear and cougar their father used a type of foxhound breed called a Bluetick. These had sense to stay away from these dangerous predators.

When the price on wolf and coyote went up he continued to hunt these with the Blueticks. They were admirable tracking dogs and were capable of running their prey all day. They were, however, very slow for they rarely came in range of the wolves and coyotes. Their father mated a greyhound bitch to a large scent hunting breed of unknown origin—from the description it was probably a staghound. The progeny had speed to catch up with the quarry and were slipped when the trail became hot. They were useless for bear and cougar however as they ran silent and attacked the quarry. The result had to be disembowelled and dead dogs, for smaller game however, they seemed to be quite good. Their extinction came about in a most peculiar way. Rattle snakes abounded in the dry areas Baines hunted. His hounds avoided them like the plague, but his greyhound hybrids never seemed to learn the knack of keeping clear of them. One by one they were bitten by rattle snakes and died. He never lost one Bluetick hound during his entire period of time in Texas. Gradually the predators decreased and when old man Baines went into retirement there was no work for his sons. Both went into coal mining as had their grandfather in Doncaster. The turn of the century saw the last of the famous predator hunters. The cougar and bear became rare and the wolf went close to extinction. Only the coyote, the wild dog of the desert, hung on to a precarious existence living where a rat would find difficulty in surviving. The Baines brothers, now quite old, still hunt the coyote with their pack of mongrel greyhounds, but they still tell the wonderful tales their father told them of when Texas was a wild untamed land. Now towns exist where their father hunted wild razorback pig and a shopping precinct stands where old man Baines treed a large cougar. Times changed and not always for the better.

Australia also made use of a number of greyhound crosses. Kangaroos ate much of the grass needed for sheep farming. Furthermore the kangaroos cropped the grass so low that sheep could not feed. In the early days of colonisation, kangaroos were a plague. Settlers made use of existing dogs and crossed them with greyhounds and allied blooded dogs Wolfhounds, Deerhounds, Staghounds and Foxhounds were used in their creation of a new and very game breed, the Kangaroo hound, a breed which was kept only for work, was never standardised and probably never bred true. A kangaroo can rip a dog asunder with a savage kick of the hind legs and dogs learnt how to pull over this ungainly creature quickly or never survived the first hunt. Furthermore the dingo, or wild dog of Australia bred by aborigines and running wild caused havoc among the sheep and killed newly born calves. The hybrid greyhound was required to kill these wild dogs, and bounties of sufficient size were offered to make professional predator control a profitable business. Graphic accounts of this time are written in the book " Finn, an Irish Wolfhound " which makes fascinating reading.

Ray Morgan mentions a curious cross that frequently paid off. Joe Wright of Mobberley bred some exceedingly good and very beautiful lurchers from crossing an Old English Sheepdog with a greyhound. Old English Sheepdogs were once excellent drovers dogs and their warm protective coat was in keeping with the rough life both dog and drover lived. Show breeders increased the length of the coat and produced heavily furnished heads that have so much fur that many dogs act as if they are short sighted. When trimmed they are still useful dogs. Some were used as war dogs and others of a slightly unrefined type are still used by sheep herders in some of the highlands of South Australia.